Macromedia®

Flash™ MX 2004
KillerTips

The hottest collection of cool tips and hidden secrets for Flash

Shane Elliott

Killer Tips series developed by Scott Kelby

PUBLISHER
Stephanie Wall

PRODUCTION MANAGER
Gina Kanouse

SENIOR ACQUISITIONS EDITOR
Linda Anne Bump

EXECUTIVE DEVELOPMENT EDITOR
Lisa Thibault

SENIOR PROJECT EDITOR
Sarah Kearns

COPY EDITOR
Ben Lawson

SENIOR INDEXER
Cheryl Lenser

COMPOSITION
Gloria Schurick

MANUFACTURING COORDINATOR
Dan Uhrig

COVER DESIGN AND
CREATIVE CONCEPTS
Felix Nelson

MARKETING
Scott Cowlin
Tammy Detrich
Hannah Onstad Latham

PUBLICITY MANAGER
Susan Nixon

International Standard Book Number: 0-7357-1383-9

Library of Congress Catalog Card Number: 2003411991

Printed in the United States of America

First printing: November, 2003

08 07 06 05 04 03   7 6 5 4 3 2 1

Interpretation of the printing code: The rightmost double-digit number is the year of the book's printing; the rightmost single-digit number is the number of the book's printing. For example, the printing code 03-1 shows that the first printing of the book occurred in 2003.

Trademarks

Warning and Disclaimer

To my Mom, Cheryl, whose guidance, love, and understanding

has simply made me a better man.

To Chad and Stephanie, for continually making me proud

to be their brother.

Finally, to Mammaw, whose unconditional support

has given me strength when I thought I had none left.

ACKNOWLEDGMENTS

Anytime you see an acknowledgment page in a book you think, "Oh god, here we go. The guy's gonna start kissing butt." Well, what choice do I have? In all seriousness, there are a lot of people to thank, and it's sort of like making an Oscar speech since you have to get to everyone in one page. So, I'll start out by thanking the person who made this book come to life…Me. Okay, I'm talking about Linda Bump, Senior Acquisitions Editor at New Riders. From beginning to end, she pushed without being pushy, inspired, and was just plain wonderful to work with. She owes me a coffee and I plan to collect. I'd also like to thank Lisa Thibault (development editor) and Robert M. Hall and Kim Cavanaugh (technical editors) for their swift turnaround and very warm, supportive attitudes. It's very important to feel like you're collaborating instead of being criticized, and that is certainly how I was made to feel.

Everyone I work with at OTX Research from the top down. Shelley Zalis, Kristin Luch, Amit Kzemian, and everyone in the Engineering department who make coming into the office something that I can actually look forward to, and trust me, that's a difficult thing to do.

David Fugate, my literary agent at Waterside Productions, was arguably the only reason this book came to fruition. Having a lot going on at the time, I was reluctant to believe I could make a book like this happen and happen well. David, you inspired me to forge ahead and had faith that it was possible. For that, I thank you. Have your people call my people and we'll do lunch.

Of course no one could write a book about Flash MX 2004 unless there was such a thing, so for that I'd like to thank Macromedia. Henriette Cohn and Heather Holleander specifically made getting information on the product an easy task and offered every opportunity to learn the most possible about such a great release of Flash. I would have had a hard time writing about the changes in Flash MX 2004 if it weren't for these wonderful women and the developers and engineers as a whole.

I've saved my personal thank you's for the end. Everyone has challenges in their life and none of us could overcome them without help from people who believe in us when no one else does, not even yourself. Fortunately I have several such people in my life. I'd especially like to thank Wendy Donovan for being such a source of honesty and understanding, and for her attempts at tolerating my moods. Frank Krueger, Chris Pauley, Trevor Boelter, Greg Adler, Martin Barter, and the rest of my close friends for many nights of sushi, helping me to stay creatively fulfilled, and reminding me that laughter is the root of all evil. One last thing… "I got a fever, and the only prescription is more cow bell." If you get that, then I thank you too.

ABOUT THE AUTHOR

Shane Elliott

After a long career as a student of computer sciences at several universities, including North Carolina State, Elon College, and Cal State Los Angeles, Shane's curiosity and thorough training has led him in directions even he himself could not have predicted. Although he has always been very visually oriented and creative, his skills always led him toward the more technical aspects of web and new media development.

This all changed when Shane shifted focus to design while working at a broadband search company known as Rampt. Rampt broke new ground by offering a fully functional search engine, which at the time operated completely in Flash 4. Ever since his introduction to Flash 4, Shane has followed the growth of Flash as a developing product. He has worked closely with every new release and, as a result, has been honored with awards from Macromedia Site of the Day, Invision 2000, and The Bandies 2000, as well as a nomination in the Flash Forward Film Festival in New York.

Given Shane's knowledge of programming, mixed with Flash design skills and gravitational personality, it was only a matter of time before he began to teach others the relatively new art of Flash design. While teaching at Moviola and American Media Training, he realized that sharing his knowledge with others was the next step he wanted to take. Making this a priority opened doors into authoring material for the *Flash MX Bible*, *ActionScript MX Bible*, and *The Flash Animator*. Having written screenplays, plays, and short stories throughout his career in design, the authoring bug had bitten long ago and making the transition into writing was a natural progression. Most recently, Shane partnered with long-time friend and colleague, Robert Reinhardt, to develop an online introductory course for Flash MX that is offered at universities all over the country.

In the recent past, Shane has applied his rich mixture of skills by working with a variety of clients, such as Infiniti, Energizer, Crest National, Toyota, TBWA Chiat / Day, and Saatchi & Saatchi. He continues to broaden his experiences by developing rich web and stand-alone Flash applications for private sources and hopes to continue growing in all directions that are made available to him. If there are creative avenues to be taken, Shane will continue to find and pursue each and every one of them.

If you'd like to keep up to date with what Shane is doing, visit his web site at www.timberfish.com.

ABOUT THE TECHNICAL REVIEWERS

These reviewers contributed their considerable hands-on expertise to the entire development process for *Macromedia Flash MX 2004 Killer Tips*. As the book was being written, these dedicated professionals reviewed all the material for technical content, organization, and flow. Their feedback was critical to ensuring that *Macromedia Flash MX 2004 Killer Tips* fits our reader's need for the highest quality technical information.

Kim Cavanaugh is a teacher for the School District of Palm Beach County (Florida), where he has been teaching middle-school students web design using Dreamweaver, Fireworks, and Flash since 1999. Kim is also an adjunct professor at Palm Beach Community College, where he teaches Dreamweaver and Flash.

The author of two beginner's guide titles for Dreamweaver and Fireworks (Osborne/McGraw-Hill), Kim has also developed course materials for the Learning Library (UK) and contributed to the *Macromedia Studio MX Bible* (Wiley). Kim has contributed numerous articles to Macromedia DevNet and writes extensively for Community MX.com, covering the full range of Studio MX products.

Prior to beginning his career as an educator, Kim worked for ten years as a custom furniture designer and manufacturer, and was a Field Artillery officer in the U.S. Army. He is a graduate of Stetson University (Deland, Florida), with a degree in Political Science.

Kim lives in West Palm Beach with his wife and daughter and loves all things associated with life in South Florida—especially warm weather, the Miami Dolphins, in-shore fishing, and Jimmy Buffett tunes.

A native of Fort Lauderdale, Florida, **Robert M. Hall** has been involved with computers and technology for more than 20 years in several fields, ranging from design and prepress work to enterprise-level architecture and programming of next-generation ATM machines, kiosks, coin counters, and wireless applications for financial and banking industries. Robert maintains his own corporate entity, Feasible Impossibilities, through which he does contract work and speaking engagements. He also maintains a web site covering Flash-related news, articles, and a personal blog of his projects and items of interest. The all-Flash version is available at `www.impossibilities.com`, and his html-based blog is available at `www.impossibilities.com/blog`. Robert's published work can be found in chapters he contributed to the books *Flash MX Magic* and *Flash Enabled*, both published by New Riders; a chapter in the *Flash MX Bible*, published by Wiley; and several online articles for InformIt.com. Robert also contributed to the development of the exams currently in use by Macromedia for both Flash 5 and Flash MX Certified Professional programs. His most recent work can be found in an article written for the Flash Development Center on Macromedia DevNet located at `www.macromedia.com/devnet/mx/flash/articles/amfphp.html`.

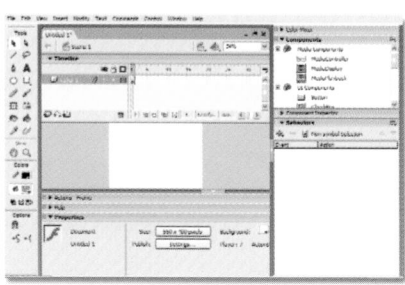

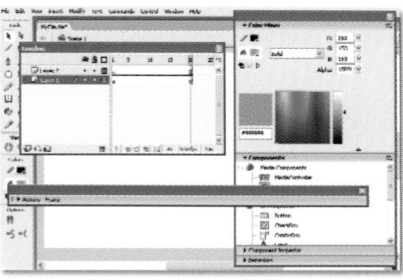

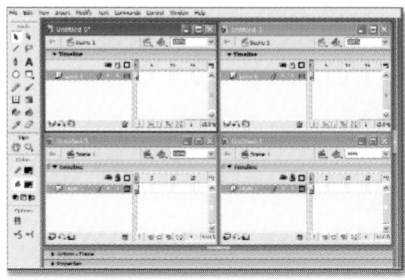

TABLE OF CONTENTS

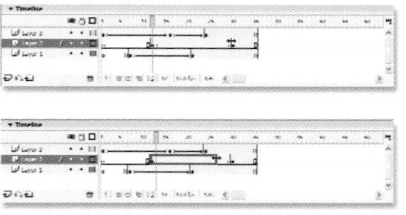

TABLE OF CONTENTS

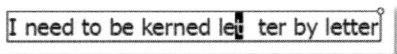

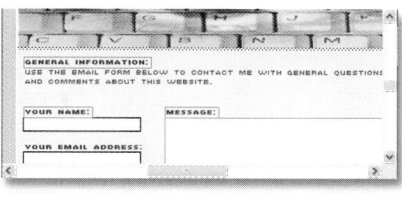
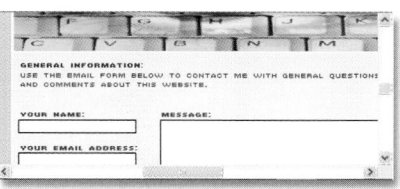
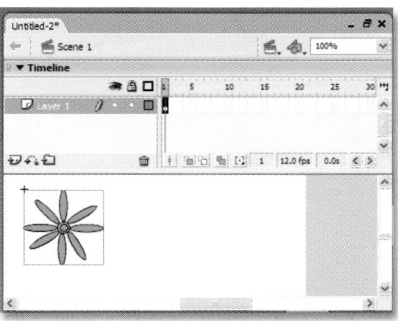

TABLE OF CONTENTS

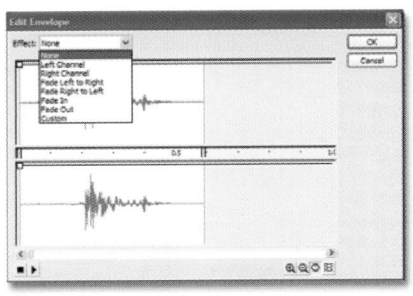

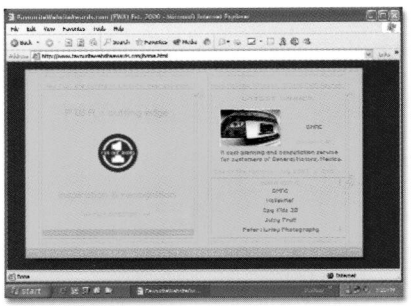

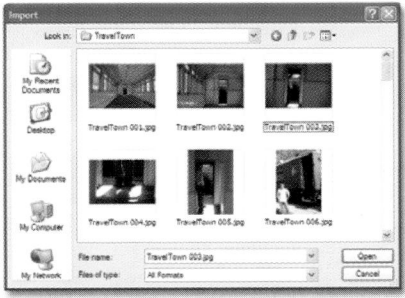

TABLE OF CONTENTS

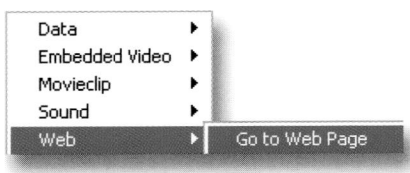

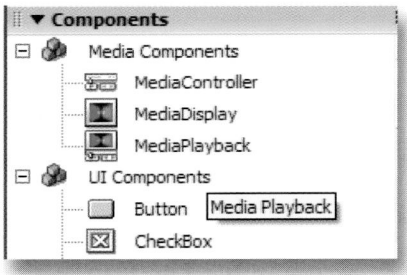

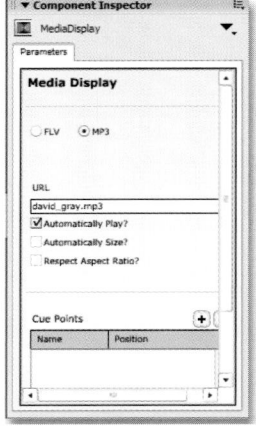

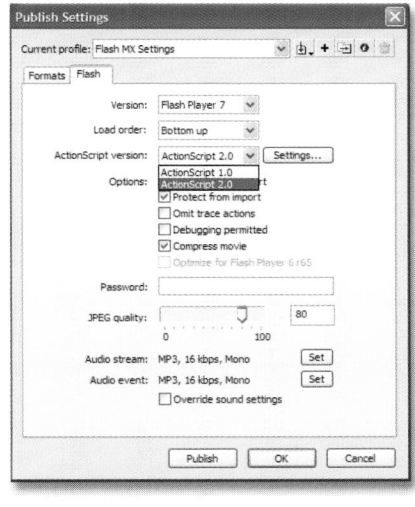

TABLE OF CONTENTS

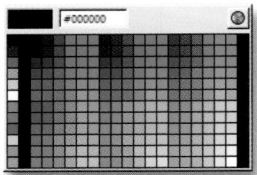

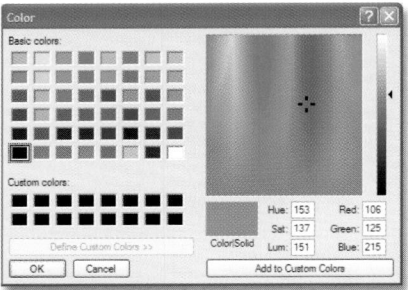

TELL US WHAT YOU THINK

As the reader of this book, you are the most important critic and commentator. We value your opinion and want to know what we're doing right, what we could do better, what areas you'd like to see us publish in, and any other words of wisdom you're willing to pass our way.

As Senior Acquisitions Editor for New Riders Publishing, I welcome your comments. You can fax, email, or write me directly to let me know what you did or didn't like about this book—as well as what we can do to make our books stronger. When you write, please be sure to include this book's title, ISBN, and author, as well as your name and phone or fax number. I will carefully review your comments and share them with the author and editors who worked on the book.

Please note that I cannot help you with technical problems related to the topic of this book, and that due to the high volume of email I receive, I might not be able to reply to every message.

Fax: 317-428-3280

Email: linda.bump@newriders.com

Mail: Linda Bump
           Senior Acquisitions Editor
           New Riders Publishing
           800 East 96th Street, 3rd Floor
           Indianapolis, IN 46240 USA

INTRODUCTION

Why I Wrote This Book

It's a funny story, actually. I was sitting alone in my apartment having just watched *Terms of Endearment* for the fifth time, and I was still crying when the phone rang. It was the President. He said, "Shane, I need to ask you a favor. I need you to write a book and I need that book to change the world." I replied, "I'll do it, but I need to know all about Area 51, one hundred thousand dollars, and a lifetime subscription to *Marie Claire*." Okay, so one out of three ain't bad. After I finished looking at the alien bodies, I got right to work on this book.

So, there is an actual reason that I wrote this book. This series of books created by Scott Kelby already includes two other programs that I use on a regular basis: Dreamweaver and Photoshop. To be honest, I had only heard of the *Killer Tips* series of books and had never read one at all. When I was told that an opportunity to write one was coming up, I was a little apprehensive. I had no idea of the content or what such a book would require of me. After looking over the Dreamweaver and Photoshop books that had come before, the decision was easy. I thought, "Flash designers need a book like this!" Actually, if nothing else, I wanted to compile all the tips I had run across or discovered in my years of using Flash so that I could have a quick reference. Let's face it: When you read through a magazine, the first thing you look at is the photos or the balloon text in the margins of *Marie Claire*. Well, you won't find anything in the margins of this book because everything in it is a margin tip. The entire book is just a collection of Flash tips that will help you work better and faster, and ultimately get a call from the President yourself.

Is This Book for You?

I don't know how this book wouldn't be for you. I know every author toots his own horn this way, but honestly I wrote a book that, had someone else written it, I would want to own. When it comes to Flash, we all know that the program is ever-expanding and continually becoming more complex. That means more shortcuts to get things done. Since there are so many tips like this, I always had a hard time remembering them all or at least remembering to use them all. So to be honest, this book is as much for me as it is for you. Which is kind of strange. I mean, I'm sitting working, and then I go to my own book as a reference.

I know what you're saying. "Where can I get a free subscription to *Marie Claire*?" Well, maybe I can put in a good word for you with the White House. In the meantime, try asking yourself this question instead… "If Flash is so huge and robust, couldn't you have put in 10,000 tips?" Of course I could have. I could have made every little shortcut in the entire program into a tip, but then the book would be 3,000 pages and very hard to flip through or use as a reference. What I've done is chosen the tips that have always helped and excited me. These are what I consider to be "Killer Tips."

There were many times while writing that I would come across a tip that I always knew, but just seldom used. I actually became excited while rediscovering them, and I think whether you are discovering or rediscovering them, you will too. Because the book was written to be a collection of the best tips for everyone, from the beginner to the expert, I know for a fact this book is for you. If it's not for you, go ahead and buy it just to make sure.

Okay, How Do I Begin?

Start by taking out a fresh envelope, putting $1,000 inside, and sending it to New Riders c/o Shane Elliott. Okay, now you're ready to start the book. Actually, as with any other book, you might think you should begin by flipping to the first page of the tips and going from there. However, this book was not intended to be read straight through. Ultimately, I wrote the book to be a categorized collection of tips, and you can jump from one page to the next to find the kind of stuff you need without having to read through the entire book. You don't need any special software (other than Flash MX 2004, of course); there's no CD-ROM included with a bunch of tutorials that can be confusing and hard to manage.

Keep in mind that I spell out each step for each tip, so if you're an avid Flash user, don't get frustrated if you see (CTRL-F8) every time I mention converting something to a symbol. The tips are designed to operate completely on their own, and most of them don't require you to even have read anything else in the book to be effective. Just flip to any page of the book and start applying these useful hints. It's as simple as that.

Is This Book for Macintosh, Windows, or Both?

Because there's no CD-ROM or any additional software required, this book is for any and all Flash MX 2004 users. Because this release of Flash MX runs under OS X on the Mac side, you'll need to have that, but I'm sure you figured that out when you bought the program. Of course since Flash looks slightly different on the Mac than on a PC, you will notice that some of your screens may not be identical to mine, but luckily Macromedia has made sure that Flash works exactly the same on the Mac as it does on Windows. The only true variations you'll see is that the keyboard shortcuts are different. But, guess what…I actually put in both sets of shortcuts throughout. How about that? You love me, right?

How to Use This Book

This book can be used for many different things. You can put it on your coffee table to increase your social status amongst friends. You can use it to even out a lopsided table. You can roll it up and smack someone in the head. Or, you can actually read the thing every now and then. I'd recommend the latter. What I do is just make sure this is with me when I work. When it's by my side, I feel like I can always jump to a page and find just the thing I need. I hope you will find this, too.

Make sure to check out `www.killerflashtips.com`, where you can find copy updates, corrections, and even additional tips that are discovered after the book's release.

What Not to Do

There's one thing that you must never do when reading this book. I mean it—this is really, really important, and if you do this, you may never be the same again. I saw one guy do this thing, and he just ended up sitting in his chair and drooling on himself for the years that followed. It was really strange and I can't quite explain it, but take my word for it. Don't go flipping through my book looking for sidebar tips. They just aren't there. Because the entire book is sidebar tips. Oh, and don't ever tell anyone about my *Marie Claire* subscription. It's personal and people might get the wrong idea.

Flash MX 2004 Killer Tips
Edited by Scott Kelby

Welcome to *Flash MX 2004 Killer Tips*. As Editor for the Killer Tips series, I can't tell you how excited and truly gratified I am to see this concept of creating a book that is cover-to-cover nothing but tips, extend from my original book (*Photoshop Killer Tips*) into *Flash MX 2004 Killer Tips*.

The idea for this series of books came to me when I was at the bookstore looking through the latest Photoshop books on the shelf. I found myself doing the same thing to every book I picked up: I'd turn the page until I found a paragraph that started with the word "Tip." I'd read the tip, then I'd keep turning until I found another sidebar tip. I soon realized I was hooked on tips, because I knew that if I were writing the book that's where I'd put all my best material. Think about it: If you were writing a book, and you had a really cool tip, an amazing trick, or an inside secret or shortcut, you wouldn't bury it among hundreds of paragraphs of text. No way! You'd make it stand out: You'd put a box around it, maybe put a tint behind it, and if it was really cool (and short and sweet), you'd get everybody's attention by starting with the word "Tip!"

That's what got me thinking. Obviously, I'm not the only one who likes these tips, because almost every software book has them. There's only one problem: There's never *enough* of them. And I thought, "Wouldn't it be great if there were a book that was nothing but those cool little tips?" (Of course, the book wouldn't actually have sidebars, since what's in the sidebars would be the focus: nothing but cool shortcuts, inside secrets, slick ways to do the things we do everyday, but faster—and more fun— than ever!) That was the book I really wanted, and thanks to the wonderful people at New Riders, that's the book they let me write (along with my co-author and good friend Felix Nelson). It was called *Photoshop Killer Tips*, and it became an instant bestseller because Felix and I were committed to creating something special: A book where every page included yet another tip that would make you nod your head, smile, and think "Ahhh, so that's how they do it."

If you've ever wondered how the pros get twice the work done in half the time, it's really no secret: They do everything as efficiently as possible. They don't do *anything* the hard way. They know every timesaving shortcut, every workaround, every speed tip, and as such they work at full speed all the time. They'll tell you, when it comes to being efficient, and when it comes to staying ahead of the competition: Speed Kills!

Well, what you're holding in your hand is another Killer Tips book: A book packed cover-to-cover with nothing but those cool little sidebar tips (without the sidebars). Shane Elliot has captured the spirit and flavor of what a Killer Tips book is all about. I can't wait for you to get into it, so I'll step aside and let him take the wheel, because you're about to get faster, more efficient, and have more fun in Flash MX 2004 than you ever thought possible.

Have fun and enjoy the ride!

All my best,

Scott Kelby, Series Editor

I'll Lay You Out

Organize It

Have you ever opened your closet door and realized that it looks as though you pick your clothes by flailing your arms about and choosing the only outfit left on the

I'll Lay You Out

Tips on Organizing Your Workspace

rack? Okay, maybe you're more organized than I am, but if you're like any of my friends, then you're not—so stop lying. Oh, your closet is pristine? Okay, what about your car? That too? Oh, well, that's pretty impressive. Anyhow, now that I'm officially writing nonsense, let me say that this chapter is for the sloppy as well as for the Virgo god of cleanliness. You see, all I do through this entire section is give you tips on how to make the best use of the space you're given. Let's face it—the Flash interface doesn't please everyone. In fact, it has driven some of my friends to drink. Wait, that was me that drove them to the bar. Anyway, whether you like the interface or hate it, you'll love this chapter because it helps you make Flash what you want it to be.

 WHERE SHOULD I PUT THE TIMELINE?

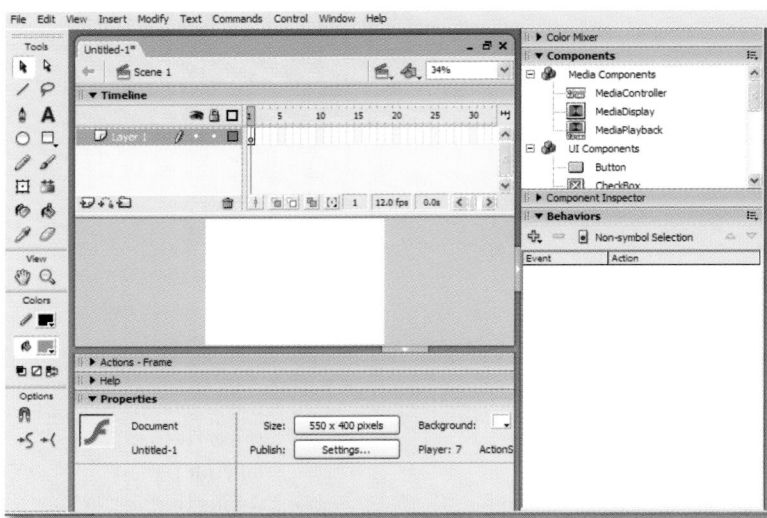

After working in Flash for awhile, you may have rearranged your panels yourself, or you may have used one of the predefined panel sets, and you might be thinking to yourself, "The Timeline doesn't seem to be in the best place." If that's the case, here's a suggestion.

Place your Timeline above your Stage so that the only things to the left and right of it are the Toolbar and the main column of panels. The reason for this is that you want to be able to scroll across your Timeline using the horizontal scrollbar along the bottom. Sometimes putting the Timeline in the wrong place can vastly limit scrolling or even prevent it entirely. This is especially helpful if you have hundreds of frames on a particular timeline. The alternative to this would be to continually restructure your layout each time you want to scroll your Timeline. Hey, if that's what you want to do, then fine, don't listen to me (kidding).

 ## I NEED MY SPACE!

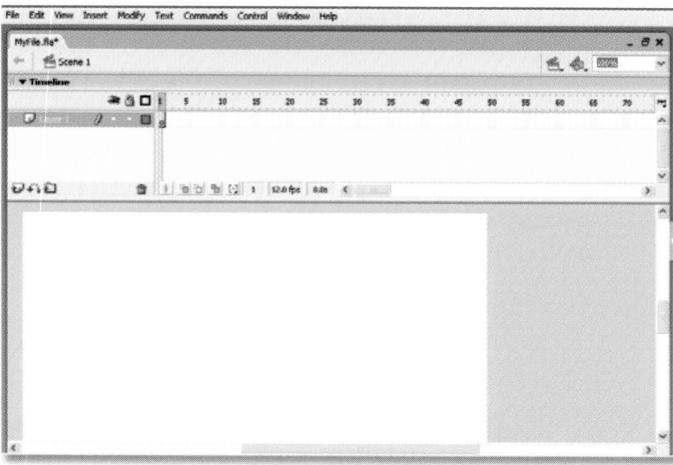

Yes, panels are a wonderful thing, and we need them to be available to us at all times. Well, almost. If you have limited screen real estate or you work on very large files, you may be unable to view your Stage at 100% without cutting off some of the Stage from your view. If this is ever the case, just press F4 to quickly hide all your panels. The only things that remain are your Stage and your Timeline (which you can collapse). The best thing about this is that you can get all those precious panels back any time by pressing F4 again. I have to say, I use this little trick most of all.

   IT'S MY WAY OR THE HIGHWAY

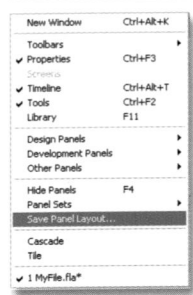

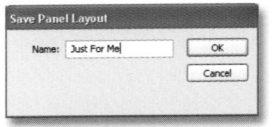

I know all of you love panels. They are always placed perfectly on your screen and the exact panel you need is always readily available. But for those of you who like to do things your way, read on. True, you get a default panel layout, but you can also make your own. After you have all the panels you want open and in the places you like, go to Window > Save Panel Layout. Enter a simple name for your panel layout, such as "Just For Me," and click OK. The next time you go to Panel Sets, you'll see your new panel set waiting for you. You can also overwrite a panel set by saving with the same exact name as an existing one. If anything ever goes wrong, you're only a couple clicks away from happiness.

Removing a custom set is a little more difficult. You'll need to go to your Configuration > Panel Sets folder and remove the set you no longer want. Finding this folder can be tricky because its location differs depending on what OS you're using.

Note the special locations for different operating systems. For Windows 2000 or XP, go to C:\Documents and Settings\<username>\Local Settings\Application Data\Macromedia\Flash MX 2004\en\Configuration\Panel Sets. For Windows 98 or ME, go to C:\WINDOWS\Application Data\Macromedia\Flash MX 2004\en\Configuration\Panel Sets.

And for Macintosh OS X, go to <Macintosh HD>:<username>:Library:Application Support:Macromedia:Flash MX 2004:en:Configuration:Panel Sets.

   HEY, HEY, HEY, GOODBYE

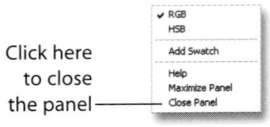

Click here
to close
the panel

So adding panels to your layout is fairly straightforward, but removing one might not be. Sure, you could always just uncheck the panel listed in the Window menu, but panels aren't always listed just there. Instead of going through all the menus to find what caused a panel to appear, just go straight to the source of your angst. To remove any individual panel from your interface, simply expand the panel (it cannot be collapsed when doing this), go to the menu at the top right of the panel, and click and choose Close Panel. Now that panel has been removed from your life forever. Well, at least until you enable it again.

  ## SHRINKING SECTIONS

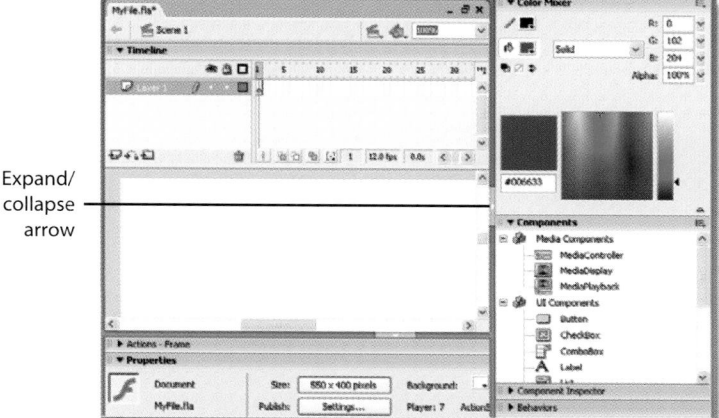

Expand/
collapse
arrow

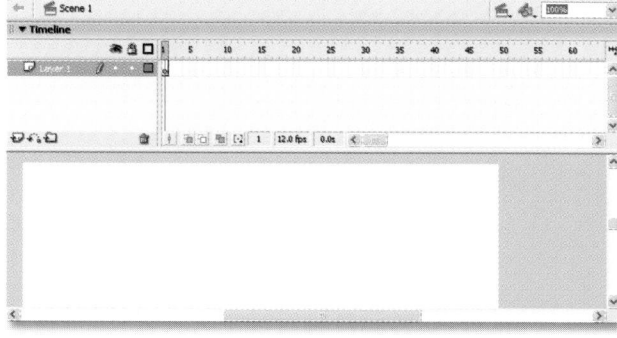

The introduction of dockable panels in Flash MX was a great improvement over previous panel designs in Flash. Dockable panels provided much more control over what the user sees and how he or she sees it. Still it wasn't perfect. For instance, you could never get rid of that main column of panels without removing them all or hiding every panel in the program. Neither way was quite right. Flash MX 2004 introduces what can best be described as collapsible sections of the interface. Now you'll notice that the dividing bar between certain areas of the interface (that panel column, for example) has a very thin arrow button. This will look familiar, as it could be seen in the Actions Panel, Debugger, and other parts of Flash MX. Now that it's part of the interface itself, using this button can completely collapse that section of the interface, leaving you with a lot more room and access to other important areas of the program. Nice improvement indeed.

   EVERYONE'S AFLOAT

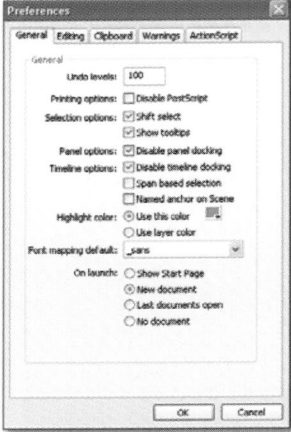

Some people actually miss the old style interfaces where all the panels floated around the application instead of eating up space by being docked. As mentioned earlier, there are several ways to free up space by hiding panels and whatnot, but if you're really gunning for all your panels to float, then you can have it your way.

Use CTRL-U (Flash > Preferences on Mac) to bring up your Flash preferences, and then switch to the General tab. Now simply put a check by "Disable panel docking" and "Disable timeline docking," click OK, and bam, floating panels. The only thing left docked is the Toolbar, which you can undock by dragging it by its handle (little dots in the top-left corner). Be aware that this tip is only really helpful when your resolution is set to 1024×768 or higher; otherwise, it just creates clutter. To get your panels back to docked mode, uncheck the two boxes and choose the Default Panel Set from Window > Panel Sets.

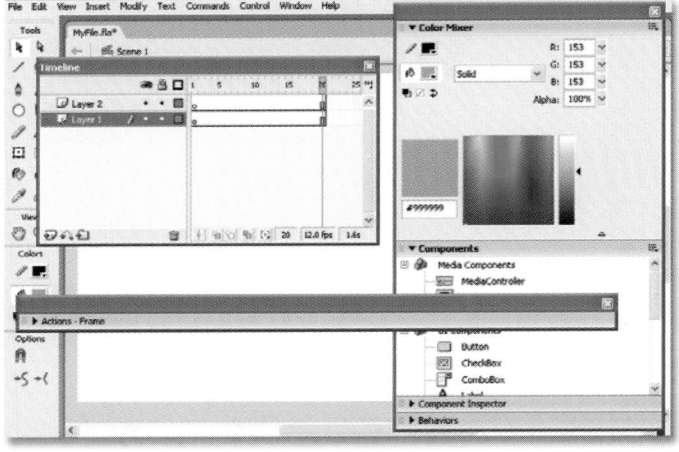

IT'S TIME TO REMOVE THE TIMELINE

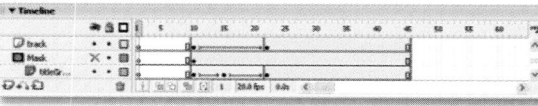

Okay, so every now and then when you're not doing much in the way of animation, the Timeline can simply get in your way. A quick remedy to this dilemma is to remove it. Because there's no way to close it using its panel menu at the top right (it doesn't have one), there is a shortcut instead. Use CTRL-ALT-T (CMD-OPT-T on Mac) to hide the Timeline, and then the same to show it again when you're ready to accept it back into your life.

   THE LIBRARY WON'T SIT STILL

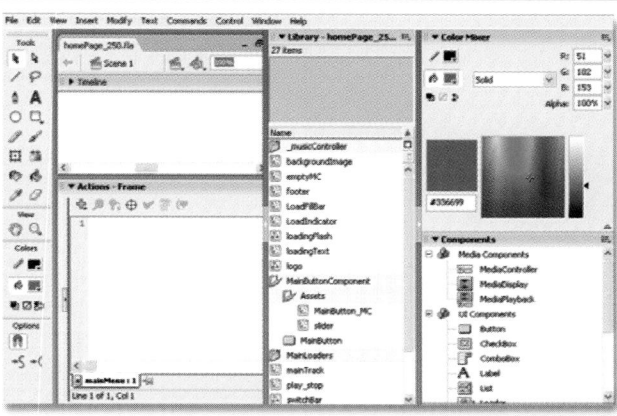

Typically when you call upon Flash to display your Library (CTRL/CMD-L), that darn thing wants to float around your screen. This can get annoying if it is covering valuable items such as your Stage or other panels that you may need to watch while working. But if you're like me, you like having your Library handy every now and then. Well, the Library is completely dockable, just like all the other panels and windows in Flash MX 2004. To dock your Library, just grab the top-left corner of it (where all the little dots are) and drag it over another docked panel or inspector until it snaps. And if you have enough screen real estate, you can even dock it to the left of your panels that run down the right side of the Flash interface. Either way, it's a much better option than continually moving it out of the way or constantly resizing it so you can see what you're doing.

NAME YOUR LAYERS

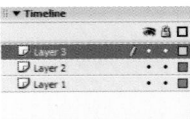 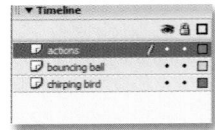

As you add more layers to your document, you'll want to start distinguishing them from each other. Flash attempts to do this for you by giving themselves names like "Layer 1" and "Layer 2," but that will only take you so far.

Eventually you'll want to begin naming each layer according to what you have on them. So if you have a ball bouncing on a layer, you can give it a name like "Bouncing Ball" to keep track. To change the default name of any layer, double-click the current layer name and type what you want.

Believe me, after you have twenty well-named layers on a given timeline, you'll look back to this tip and say, "Thank you, Shane! You're my new best friend." Either that or you won't.

HIDDEN LAYER NAME...

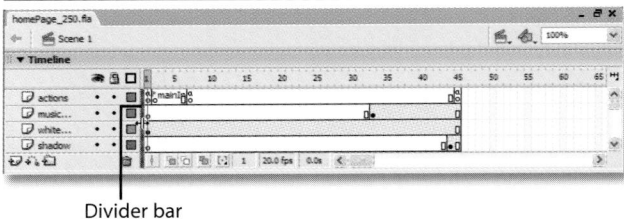

Divider bar

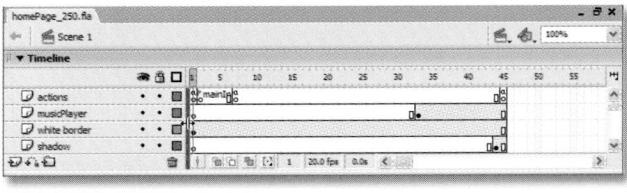

It's considered good practice to name your different layers according to what you have on each one. Being the good little developer that you are, you probably ran into a common issue when naming your layers. When you assign a layer a name that is too long to be viewed, Flash will just display what it can and place a few dots at the end to let you know that the name goes on. You could always shorten your layer names, but it seems rather unfair that you should be limited this way. Instead, grab the bar separating the layer names from the frames and drag it to the right until you see your layer names.

The only problem with this trick is that the position of the dividing bar won't stick after you move it. That means you'll have to do this every time you open the file. Saving the panel layout won't help either, I'm afraid.

  I'M TILING TO COMPARE

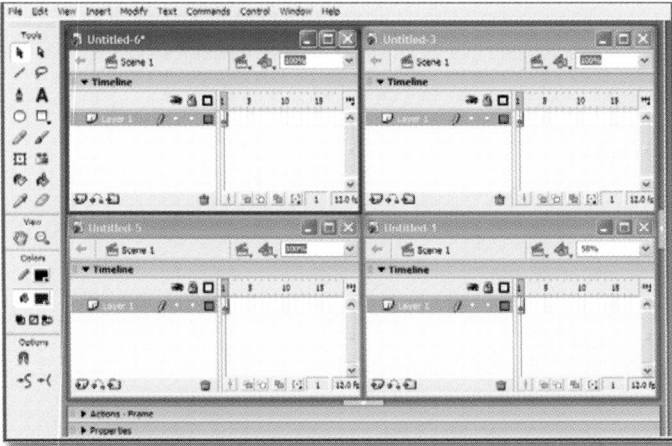

Although I'm under no delusion that tiling windows is a new or exciting concept, I will say that not many people understand why you would ever want to do such a thing. Especially when you can maximize your window to see everything, and with the new tabbing system (not available on Macs) added to Flash MX 2004, you could switch from one open document to another fairly quickly (especially after reading this book). There is a very useful purpose for tiling your open documents: to compare them side-by-side and see several of them all at once. Choosing Window and then Tile will arrange your open documents so that they are all visible at the same time. There are some things to consider when doing this: You can tile as many open documents as you wish, although I'd recommend staying under eight unless you have a theatre for a screen. Any minimized windows will stay that way and will not be included in the tiling. After you have your open documents laid out before you, it will be easy to compare them or, more importantly, copy and paste from one to the next with a simple drag-n-drop.

  A CASCADE EFFECT

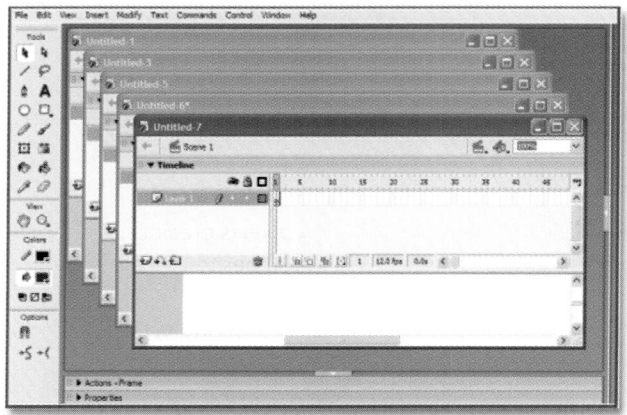

Here's another way to organize your open documents that may be just your cup of tea. Choose Window, then Cascade, and Flash will organize all open documents so that they are laid out stacked on one another but slightly offset so you can easily move between them. Any document you select comes to the front, and you're not dealing with constantly resizing your document windows to see what you want. Each open document is nicely arranged and even the same size. I myself still prefer using the new tab method, but this is an alternative for those of a different mind. If you want to return to a maximized document view, all you have to do is maximize any of the open documents, and you're back to normal. Hey, take a chance, you might like it.

   SPEEDY DOCUMENT DISPLAY

Even with today's high-end computers, certain scenes in Flash can take a lot of work for a computer to render quickly. If you have a very involved scene with a lot of artwork, components, or other complex items and you want to reposition things quickly, then you could have problems.

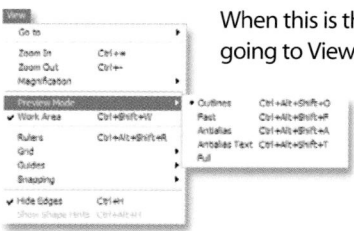

When this is the case, switch your document Preview Mode to Outlines by going to View>Preview Mode and selecting Outlines. This will render all artwork on your Stage as outlines only, allowing you to quickly position items. If you still work on an older computer, this trick will be especially handy. After you have made your changes, you can switch to another mode to get a better sense of what the final version will look like. This is just a document view, so publishing in either mode will not affect the final SWF's quality or appearance. You can also use Fast mode to get a speedy and somewhat accurate preview. Try each mode to see what's best for you and your system.

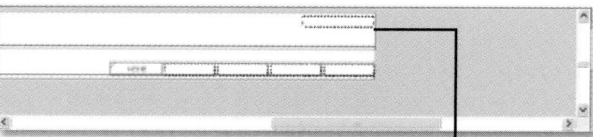

The Stage in Outline Preview mode

DOCK/UNDOCK

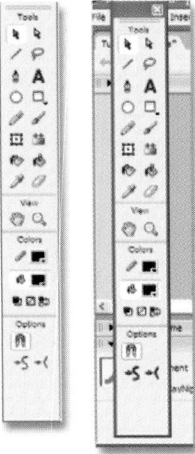

I remember when I worked at this one design firm. They set me up with a supercharged P4 and two 24-inch flat screen displays. Although this dream situation only lasted a couple of weeks, one thing I remember is that I never had to shrink or move any panels in Flash. Everything was visible at once. But let's face it, this isn't the typical designer's setup.

When it comes to screen real estate, every pixel is precious. One of the big space-wasters can be the Toolbar. It stretches to the bottom of the interface no matter what. If you ever need to quickly undock it and move it, simply double-click its little dotted handle. Drag it where you want, and then you can re-dock it by double-clicking it again. It's sent right back to the last place you docked it, and there's no dragging around to find the right place to drop it.

Sorry Mac users—this one only applies to Windows. The Flash Toolbar on Macs doesn't dock as it's always floating around.

FAMILIARITY ANYONE?

This book spends a lot of time talking about keyboard shortcuts and other time-saving operations. However, we haven't yet talked about setting up something familiar. For many of us, toolbars are what we're used to. Look at MS Word for example.

Of course we have the drawing toolbar, but there are others as well. Go to Window > Toolbars and enable both the Main and Controller toolbars.

These two toolbars will bring back familiar tools like Save and Open, as well as a very handy VCR-style controller for your Timeline. Use this to control the playback of your active Timeline without having to export or publish. The playback won't be as accurate, but it certainly helps. Sometimes it just feels good when you see old friends.

   THE HEIGHTS

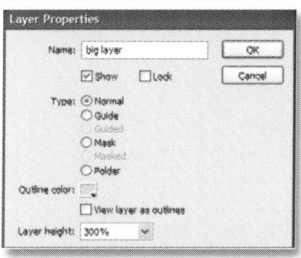

In other areas of the book, we've talked a lot about layers and frames and how to change the amount of vertical and horizontal viewing space. So far, all these view options for the Timeline have been pretty much universal—they apply to every layer or every frame. There is one thing we've left out, though—the Layer Height property.

Double-clicking a layer icon will bring up the Layer Properties window. At the bottom, you're able to set the height to 100%, 200%, or 300%. The setting is for that layer only, which can really make it stand out. There are many reasons you might want to use this setting, so we'll leave that up to you. Basically, this will just do what it says and nothing more.

   SIMPLIFY THE COLOR MIXER

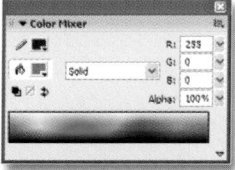

When you open Flash MX 2004 for the first time, you won't even see the Color Mixer (Window > Design Panels > Color Mixer). But if you're a designer, you'll find and open this guy right away. That being the case, you may notice that the Color Mixer can take up a lot of screen space. Sure, you could hide the entire thing by clicking its title bar, but you may want it handy without having to toggle its visibility every time.

With the Color Mixer open, click the tiny up arrow located at the bottom right to shrink it to a basic view. This saves space, and you don't have to completely hide the thing. Click the down arrow in the same spot to view the advanced features again.

PROPERTY INSPECTOR—MORE THAN MEETS THE EYE!

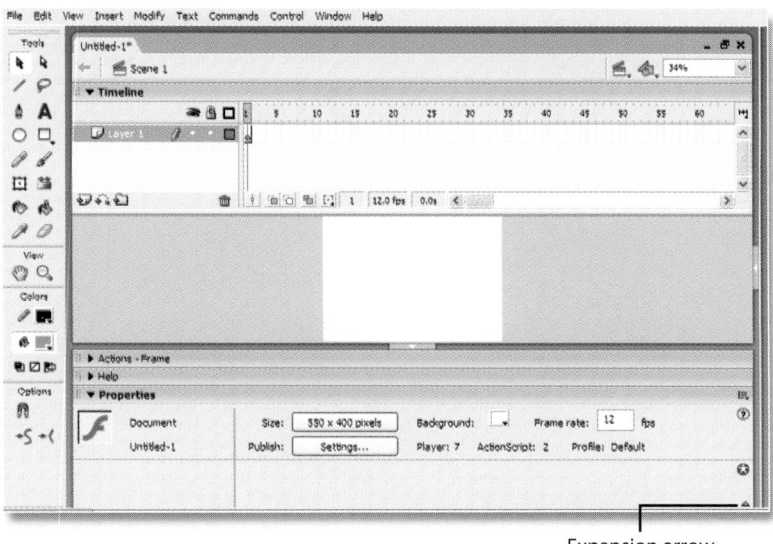

Expansion arrow

The Property inspector is just that—a place to look at the properties of what you have selected in your Flash document. Most of the time it does its job, and you would ask for nothing more from it. However, on occasion (depending on what you have selected) there can be more properties to see. Look to the bottom-right corner of the Property inspector and you'll see a tiny down arrow. If you click on it, the inspector expands, revealing even more properties.

Perhaps the best example of how useful this can be would be to select a text block that's on your Stage. Looking to the Property inspector while it's expanded gives you a whole slew of additional options. The same concept applies to many selectable elements of your Flash document, and if you ever need to reclaim the extra space, you can simply click the same arrow (now facing up) again to collapse the extra properties. When you start Flash, the Property inspector is already expanded, so feel free to collapse it to save some room.

   NEW WINDOW

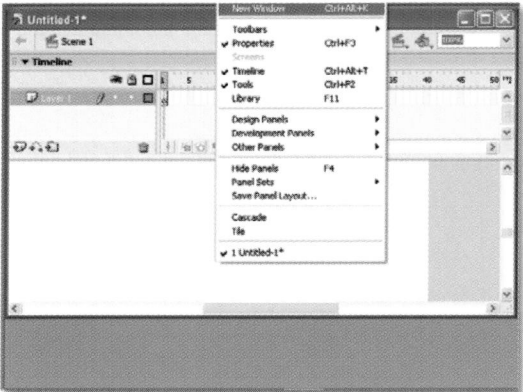

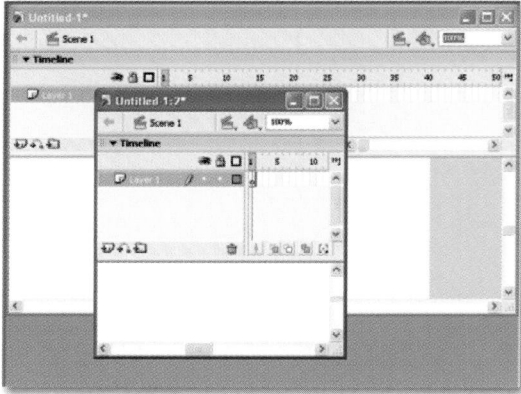

This one may throw you a bit at first. Everyone knows how to create new documents by going to File > New, but a new window is slightly different. Actually, it's a lot different. A new window is just a new view or window that displays the same document.

Open any Flash document and press CTRL-ALT-K (CMD-OPT-N on Mac), or go to Window > New Window. Either way, you'll see that a new window has opened that displays the same file. This one helps me a lot when I'm making little changes on multiple timelines because I can just open a new window and use each window to view a separate timeline. Then I can switch between them using the Quick Switch Tabber tip without having to waste time navigating between them using a single window. I must admit, this isn't something I use very often, but now that I'm telling all of you about it, I think I'll start using this one again. I love remembering stuff. That, and puppies.

I LOST MY PANEL

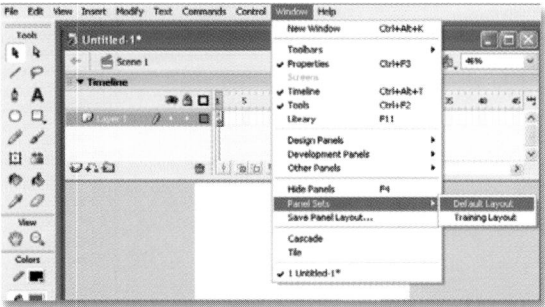

Hey, it happens from time to time. You're working and maybe you change screen resolutions with undocked panels floating around and suddenly, no matter what you do, you can't get a panel back on your screen. It has gone off into that unknown space beyond the edge of your screen. I like to call this space "Non Visible Panel Land." Whatever you call it, there's a simple way to get 'em back. Go to Window > Panel Sets and choose the Default Layout. This will bring any stray panels back to "Visible Panel Land" and prevent you from freaking out any more.

If, for any reason, you can't get the panel back this way, you will need to dump your preferences (Configuration folder in Path to Excellence tip). Restart Flash after you've dumped them. If the panel still won't come back, you'll have to uninstall and reinstall Flash. Sorry, things happen.

   PATH TO EXCELLENCE

There's a lot of mention in this book—and by developers in general—about your Flash prefs (short for *preferences*). Sometimes people recommend you delete them in case of some unknown error, or sometimes you need to know where they are so you can customize your Flash experience. The only problem is that they are in a different location depending on which operating system you use. That's why I want to give you a clear list of how to find your prefs on any computer. They are now in a folder called Configuration, and here's how you find them:

Windows 2000 or XP: C:\Documents and Settings\<username>\Local Settings\Application Data\Macromedia\Flash MX 2004\en\Configuration

Windows 98 or ME: C:\WINDOWS\Application Data\Macromedia\Flash MX 2004\en\Configuration

Macintosh OS X: <Macintosh HD>:<username>:Library:Application Support:Macromedia:Flash MX 2004:en:Configuration

Now if I or anyone else mentions your Configuration folder or prefs, you'll know exactly where to go.

My Tool Belt

Tool Zone

Imagine someone asks you to build a house. This is weird because you may not be a contractor, but stranger things have happened. So you arrive at the

My Tool Belt

Tips on Using the Tools and Toolbar

property and find a huge box of tools, about thirty men with hard hats waiting for direction from you, and a couple of drunken teenagers still asleep from partying the night before. Okay, wait, that's just strange. Scratch the construction workers. So now you're left with the huge task of building a house with a box of tools and two hung-over kids. What do you do? You should read this chapter. I'm not saying it will help you in the situation I've described, but it can't hurt. The fact is that Flash is simply a tool and, like any tool, you must know how to use it so that you can build the house that you envision. That's where this chapter comes in. In it, I let you in on all the secrets to use the tools you're given in the most effective and efficient way possible. So read on, and when you're done, get started on that house.

PAINT WITH A BITMAP

There's a nifty trick in Flash that enables you to use a bitmap as a fill for everything from rectangles to brush strokes. Start by importing a bitmap of any kind, place it on the Stage, break it apart using CTRL-B, and then use the Eyedropper Tool to sample the broken-apart bitmap. You'll notice right away that the fill color in the Toolbar is now a tiny image of the bitmap. Now you can do anything with that fill as you would with any normal fill color or gradient, so have at it!

There is a little catch to this trick. If you remove the bitmap from the Library, then you will lose your special fill. So my advice to you would be…don't.

SECRET TOOLS

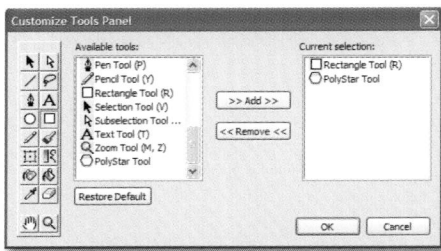

Well okay, they're not really a secret, but you can't just access them by a simple right-click on the Toolbar like you can in many applications. Flash MX 2004 has introduced a new customizable Toolbar, and there are more hidden tools than you can shake a stick at. Yes, the current Toolbar is most likely enough for anyone, but there are some very nifty new tools that are only accessible by going to Edit > Customize Tools Panel (CTRL-click on Mac). Once there, you can select any existing tool on the left and add sub tools to it. This means rearranging the toolbar any way you like. Ultimately this is just another way to customize your experience to the fullest, but if you're like me, that's exactly what you like to do anyhow.

SELECTION MAGIC

Select part of the bitmap

When you import a bitmap into Flash, you can do many things with it. Let's say you want to import a bitmap and edit that bitmap in Flash. Not possible, you say? Well, to some extent you're correct. You certainly get very limited options, but it is possible. First, import a bitmap and break it apart using CTRL-B. Next, activate the Lasso Tool and then the Magic Wand modifier. Now select any point on the bitmap and you'll notice that like colors are selected around that point. You can now do anything you want with that selected area as you would any shape in Flash.

You can also adjust the way the Magic Wand works by clicking the Magic Wand properties modifier to the right of the Wand itself. You can change the color threshold to define how closely surrounding pixel colors must match to be included in the selection, as well as adjust the smoothness of the edge of the selection. The Magic Wand only works for bitmaps that are broken apart.

   SCRAP IT!

Eraser Tool

Getting frustrated and starting over while working on anything is a common thing and nothing to be ashamed of. Right? Anyhow, while that may or may not be true, one thing is. You should never have to press two keys at once or click, drag, and then press Delete to remove everything from your Stage and start over. That's too much work for anyone. Instead just double-click the Eraser Tool at any time to quickly and effectively clear your entire Stage. Now you're back to square one. Keep in mind that as with the other methods of clearing your Stage, this will only affect layers that are not locked.

CONTROLLING THE SCALE

Scaling shape by default

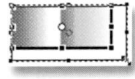

Scaling shape while holding ALT key

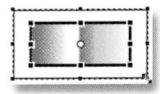

Place a shape and symbol side by side on your Stage. Now select the shape and press Q to enable the Free Transform Tool. Grabbing any handle and dragging will cause the shape to scale in the direction of the handle chosen while anchoring itself at the handle on the opposite side. If you want the shape to scale from the center point, you can hold down the ALT key. You can also hold down the SHIFT key while dragging to ensure that it scales the same amount in every direction. Now select the symbol and then press Q and you'll notice that the ALT key has the opposite effect on it because by default it scales from the center point of the symbol. The SHIFT key has the same effect on both. Now that you are aware of these little key combos, you can better control how any selected object on your Stage scales.

QUICK SCALE MCGRAW

Double-click to scale to 100%

Double-click to Show All

There are many well-known methods of scaling your document view in Flash. You can type values in, zoom in and out until it's just right, or even choose from a preset list of percentages. However, most of the time there are two main scale settings that are used over and over again. These are 100% and Show All (Show All may require less than 100% to do so). Instead of constantly choosing the Magnify/Zoom Tool and scaling your view to either of these, wouldn't it be nice to have a quick shortcut to do just that? Well, there is. From now on, you can just use the Hand Tool and Zoom Tool in the Toolbar to save a lot of time getting your workspace view just right. Simply double-click the Hand Tool at any time, from anywhere, and your view setting will be instantly set to Show All. Likewise, double-clicking on the Zoom Tool will jump your view right to 100%. It just doesn't get any easier than that.

   SPECIAL COLORS JUST FOR ME

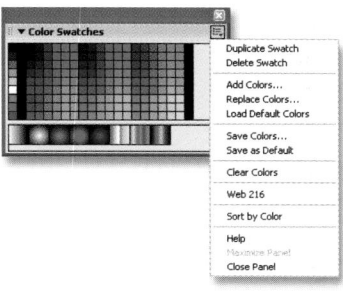

Let's say you have a site or project that has a particular color scheme that many people will use. It's doubtful that these colors will all be in the default palette, and what a pain it is to have to add the colors to everyone's color palette. Flash lets you wipe the slate clean, custom build a color palette, and then save that palette to a file, which can be shared with everyone involved.

Open the Color Swatches panel using SHIFT-F9, then click the top-right corner of the Color Swatches panel options located at the top right. To create your own palette from scratch, select Clear Colors from the list of options. Now add colors and gradients of your own by mixing the colors in the Mixer and then clicking in the Color Swatch panel when each color is ready to add.

After you've built your palette completely and have all your colors and gradients added, choose Save Colors from the panel menu and save your new color palette to a file.

Now someone else can use the Load Palette command to import your custom colors from the file you created. Neato teeto!

   FOR THE LITTLE GUYS

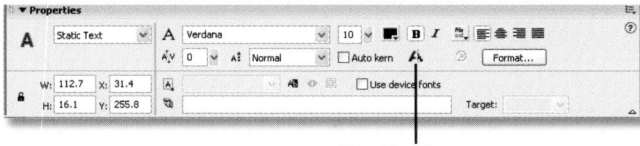

Alias Text button

Designers are continuing to use smaller and smaller fonts in their designs. Sometimes doing so gives them more room, and some of them are just excited

This text is normal.
This text is optimized.

about making visitors read their text with a loupe. Either way, if you're one of these people, you'll be glad to know that Flash MX 2004 has introduced a new option to help you optimize smaller text.

If you select any text field on your stage and look to the Property inspector, you'll notice a new button just to the right of the Auto Kern option. Clicking this new Alias Text button will toggle whether Flash applies aliasing to this text field. Aliasing is font smoothing and is often the cause of hard-to-read small text. It's recommended that you only use this option for text fields with a point size of 11 and under. Any font size bigger than that usually looks pretty good with aliasing turned on.

 STROKE AWAY

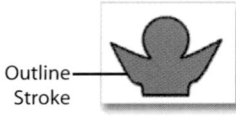

Outline —
Stroke

After playing with all the tools at your disposal, you'll often find that you have a shape with an outline that just doesn't belong anymore. Thank goodness the stroke and fill of a shape are two separate things, making it very easy to remove one or the other.

Once you have your shape drawn, just roll over the stroke of the shape and double-click it to select the entire stroke. Now press DEL on your keyboard, and away it goes.

 EYE COPY YOU

Eyedropper is
sampling the
stroke

Sampling
the fill color

Here's a quick and easy way to copy the stroke and fill attributes of one shape to another. Activate the Eyedropper Tool and roll over either the stroke or the fill of the shape you want to copy from. If you click while over the stroke, Flash will switch you to the Ink Bottle Tool and set the stroke style to match what you selected. Then just click on any part of the shape you want to apply the stroke style to and just like that, an exact copy. Do the same thing for the fill and you will have copied the style of one shape to another with hardly any trouble at all. The eyedropper only copies the style of a shape, not the shape itself. That's a whole 'nother ball of wax.

  POINT OF ROTATION

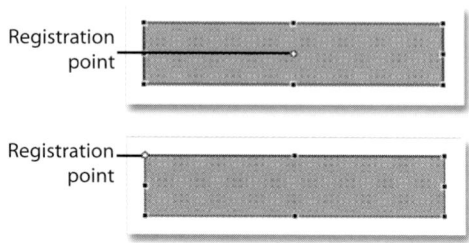

Registration point

Registration point

When rotating objects in Flash, you'll notice that they all seem to pivot on a particular point. By default, this is the center point of the object. That's fine and dandy, but for me there have been many times when I needed to rotate something in a certain way and I needed to have the pivot point be on the corner of the object. To change the pivot point of any object or shape in Flash, select the object, activate the Free Transform Tool, and move the pivot point (the little circle handle in the center) to a new location. If you move the pivot point of an object, then it will be a permanent change for that instance of the object. However, if you move the pivot point of a shape, then it will only stay there while that shape is selected. Once you unselect and reselect it you'll find the pivot back in the center again.

   PASSWORD PROTECT

Any time you go to a web site that requires you to log in to your account, you are asked for two things: a user name and password. Normally you type the user name in plain text, but when you type the password, all you see is asterisks (*) for every letter. It's a nifty little trick that's not really a trick at all, and its purpose is to increase security. You can safely type a password while someone looks on and feel secure that they don't know your login.

Guess what? Flash can do this too. Create a text field on the stage and set it to Input Text. Go to the Line Type property (where it says Single Line) and change it to Password. Test your movie (CTRL-RETURN; CMD-RETURN on Mac) and type into the text box. You'll see that each character is hidden with an asterisk. Now you can have a login page just like HTML, but completely in Flash. Isn't that exciting?

  SELECT ENTIRE SHAPE

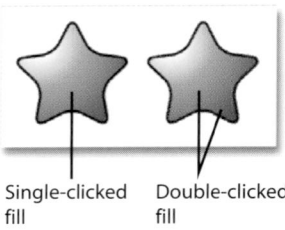

Single-clicked fill Double-clicked fill

I know, it sounds like a really hard concept to grasp, right? Something to consider is that Flash looks at a shape in two pieces: a fill and a stroke. If you have any shape on the Stage, click on its fill and then drag it. You'll see that your stroke is left behind. So, try this. To move a shape (including its stroke), double-click anywhere in the fill area of the shape. This will select the stroke and fill sections of the shape, and then you can move the entire thing at once. It can take some getting used to, but once you do, this can be a powerful way of operating.

   ROUNDING THE CORNER

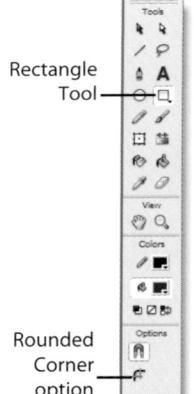

Rectangle Tool

Rounded Corner option

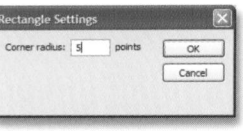

By now you know how to make a simple rectangle using the Rectangle Tool. That's fine if you want the standard right angles for your rectangle corners, but if you want something a little softer, take a look at this.

Select the Rectangle Tool and then press the Round Rectangle Radius option at the bottom of the Toolbar. Here you can set a value that will round the corners of the rectangle that you'll draw. Set it to 10 points to begin with and draw a quick rectangle. As you can see, you have nicely rounded corners now. Can you imagine trying to make these rounded corners without this little option? I know a guy who used to do it by hand over and over before discovering this one. The only thing to consider is that when you resize a rounded rectangle, the corners may appear to look less rounded. This is especially true when stretching in one direction but not the other. You may need to redraw the shape to fix that.

START FROM THE MIDDLE

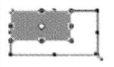

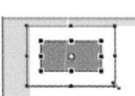

Hold down the ALT key (OPT on Mac) on your keyboard while you draw any shape in Flash MX 2004, and you'll see something slightly different. The shape is drawn out from the center at the point you clicked. Because shapes typically draw out left/up or right/down from where you click, this is a welcome little addition that can only be found in this new version of Flash.

ORIENT YOUR TEXT

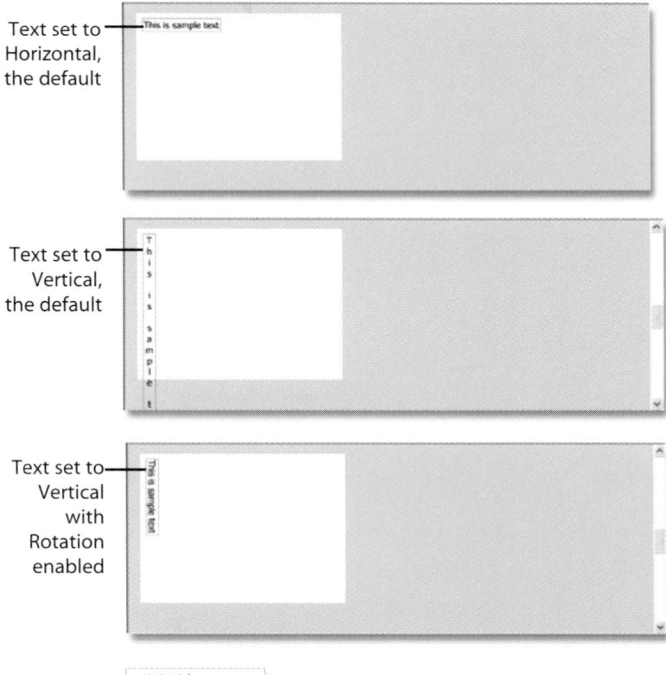

Text set to Horizontal, the default

Text set to Vertical, the default

Text set to Vertical with Rotation enabled

Setting the orientation of a text block to vertical instead of the default (horizontal) is fairly straightforward. Select your text block, go to the Property inspector, press the orientation button, and choose one of the vertical options from the list. Immediately your text field is rotated to a vertical orientation and the Rotation button found just below becomes active. Toggling this option off will actually rotate the letters in your field to appear as though you typed each letter followed by pressing ENTER (RETURN on Mac).

The beauty of it all is that no matter what orientation and rotation you set, the text field is still fully editable as if it were in its normal state. You can also continue to set the spacing and alignment for the field. Although this isn't a new feature in Flash MX 2004, it certainly works much better than it did in Flash MX.

Sorry, this one works only for Static text fields.

 TO FREE OR NOT TO FREE

Text handle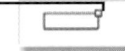

You place text blocks on the Stage using the Text Tool. When creating static text, you can place it in a free block so that it expands as you type, or in a fixed block that expands and wraps words automatically as you type.

Text handle

You can switch the text block between fixed and free modes easily by fiddling with the text block handle. To change from fixed to free, double-click the square handle (fixed block) and it switches to the round handle (free block). Alternately, if you have a free block and want it to be fixed, grab the circle handle and drag it to define the text block's size and thereby set it to be fixed.

It may be your instinct to resize a text field using the Free Transform Tool. Although this is an option, remember that this will stretch the text itself, whereas dragging the text block handle will only size the block and not the actual text.

 KEEP THAT LASSO STRAIGHT

Using lasso to select

We're not talking about the rodeo here, but this is something just as fun. Well, almost. Using the Lasso Tool is typically similar to using the Pencil Tool, where you draw your selection in free-form fashion and then proceed. But if you've ever had the need to make polygon selections, all you have to do is hold down the ALT key (OPT on Mac) while you make your selection, and you end up with nice neat lines instead of messy curves from your mouse.

Using lasso while holding ALT key

You don't have to click and drag as you normally would. Just click to start, and then click each point of your polygon selection. When you're done, double-click the last point or release the ALT key (OPT on Mac) to actually make the selection. Yeah, it's the same thing as turning on the polygon option for the tool, but with half the work. And you know what they say... "Half the work done is half the work saved." Okay, I made that up.

ONE AT A TIME, BOYS

No Color
button

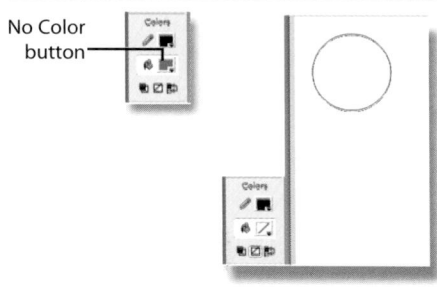

The first time you draw a shape (circle, rectangle, or other polygon), you'll be graced with a fill color and stroke color for that shape. That's great if you want an outline on everything you draw. Just for the fun of it, I'm going to ask you to do something crazy. I want you to select the Circle Tool, activate the fill color, and then press the No Color button (the middle of the three mini-buttons right under the fill). The red slash tells you that when you draw the circle, there will be no fill, and, sure enough, there isn't one. The same thing goes for the stroke, so you can draw just a circle with no outline or vice versa.

Don't try this with the Pencil Tool; it only works when drawing shapes with both fills and strokes. When I first learned Flash (back in Flash 4), I would draw strokes and fills and go back to remove the one I didn't want. Don't laugh, it's not funny.

IT'S BLACK AND WHITE

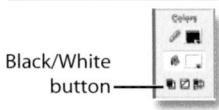

Black/White
button

There are two basic colors that everyone knows about—magenta and cyan. Wait, I mean black and white. Yeah, that's it. There may be the need to jump back to these most basic default colors, and if that need arises, here's what you do. Either in the Color Mixer panel or the Toolbar you'll see a little black and white box icon just under the fill color. Pressing this magical button will set your stroke to black and fill to white. I still wish they had a Magenta/Cyan button like that. Black and white are just so common.

SUPER SHAPER

When working with shapes, you may often need to bend them and twist them many different ways. If nothing else, it's just fun. To really mess with your shapes as if they were Play-Doh™, select one, activate the Free Transform Tool, and then enable the Envelope option (the bottom right of the four options). Several more handles appear around your selected shape. Grab any one of them and drag to see its effects. Fooling around with these little guys can yield some really cool shapes, and the best part is that it all comes out smooth, as opposed to what you get when drawing with a mouse.

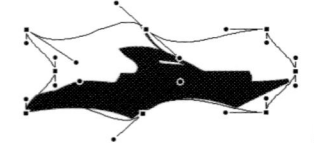

LOCK UP THOSE UNRULY GRADIENTS

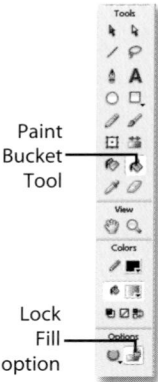

Paint
Bucket
Tool

Lock
Fill
option

Naturally, when you fill a shape using the Paint Bucket Tool, the fill is scaled to fit into that shape. This is not the only way. Draw a few shapes of various sizes in different places all over your stage. It doesn't matter which fill you use for now. Activate the Paint Bucket Tool and set your fill to a gradient or bitmap. With the Paint Bucket still active, turn Lock Fill on by pressing the right button in the option area of the Toolbar. Continue by clicking over each of the shapes on your stage and you'll see that the fill appears to spread over all the shapes instead of being scaled to fit each one. It's almost like creating a Mask, but much easier. The Lock Fill option is also available for the Paint Brush Tool, enabling you to paint as if revealing an image. Obviously this wouldn't be very helpful if you used a solid fill; it only works with a gradient or bitmap fill.

Lock Fill
enabled—Greyson

Lock Fill—Greyson
disabled

    ## SNAP TO IT

Arrow Tool

Active magnet

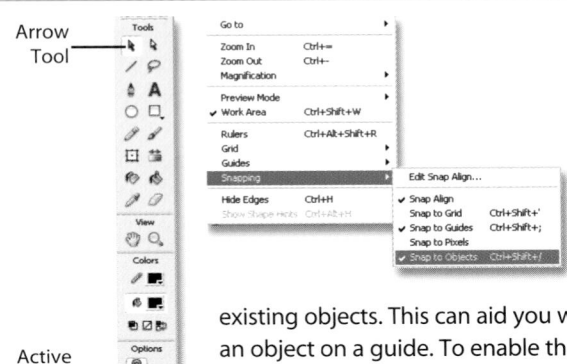

Sometimes, when you've created artwork, a symbol, or text on your Stage and you need to move it around, you want to do so freely, and other times you may want a little help from a friend. Flash allows for Object Snapping, which in effect will snap reference points of an object that you're dragging to reference points of other existing objects. This can aid you when trying to line things up or placing an object on a guide. To enable the feature, select the Arrow Tool from the Toolbar and then make sure the Snap to Objects modifier (magnet) is active. You can also enable this by going to View > Snap to Objects. Once active, you'll notice objects will snap to one another, indicated by a dark circle when you move one object close to another. For optimal use, always drag an object by its corners or center point.

      ## ONE AT A TIME, LADIES

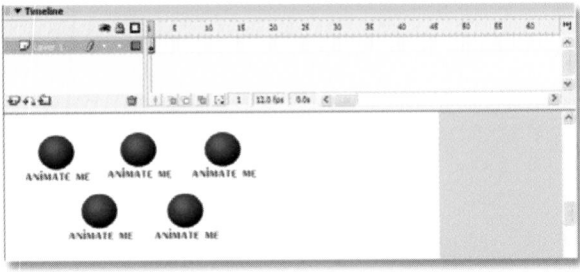

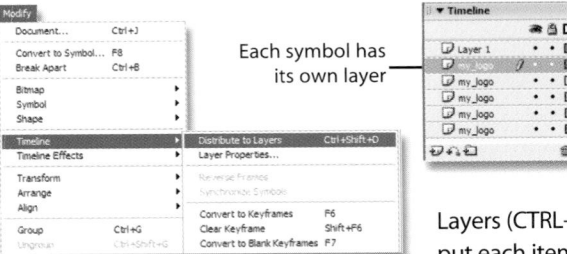

Each symbol has its own layer

As you may have figured out, if you want to animate a symbol, you have to put that symbol on its own layer by itself and then add your Motion Tween. That's all fine and good, but what if you decide to animate after you already put fifteen symbols on the same layer? Do you take a deep breath as you create a new layer for each and then copy and paste them one at a time? Let's not and say we did. The easier way is to select all the instances you want to animate at the same time, then go to Modify > Timeline > Distribute to Layers (CTRL-SHIFT-D; CMD-SHIFT-D on Mac). This will put each item you selected on its own layer all by itself so that you can animate each one individually. Flash will even name each layer to match the symbol name of each selected item. Ahhh, life is good.

  MULTIPLE SELECT

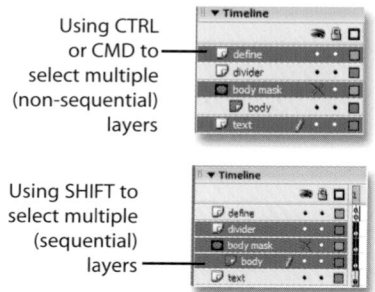

Using CTRL or CMD to select multiple (non-sequential) layers

Using SHIFT to select multiple (sequential) layers

We've all had that time where we sit back in our chair, look at our Timeline, and decide to just dump half of the layers for whatever reason. Even though there's no warning message to contend with, selecting each layer one at a time and pressing the trash icon can get tiresome. A faster way is to select multiple layers at once. You can do this two ways.

Hold down the CTRL key (CMD on Mac) while you select each layer one at a time, in any order, or hold down the SHIFT key and select a start and end layer to indicate a span of sequential layers. Either way, press the trash icon at the bottom of the Timeline to dump those selected for execution. Sorry, I didn't mean to make it sound so terminal.

   TEXT IS A CLICK OR DRAG

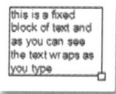 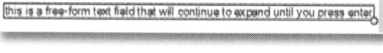

When creating text blocks in Flash, you have two types to choose from. You can add text by simply clicking any point on the stage, or by clicking and dragging to create the text block. The first method will create an auto-sizing block of text that will expand as you type and only go to the next line when you press Enter. The second method will give you a fixed text block that will auto-wrap any text you place inside according to the width of the block you created.

Both methods have their purposes, but at least you'll be able to create either one from the get-go.

   I'M HAVING A STROKE

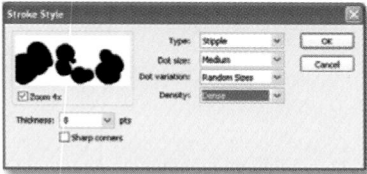

Typically when you are using outlines (strokes) on your shapes, you have a basic set of styles to choose from. For many of you, this is fine, and you've never thought twice about needing anything more. However, if you're like me (a control freak), then you'll want to be able to make your own things whenever possible. The same goes for strokes.

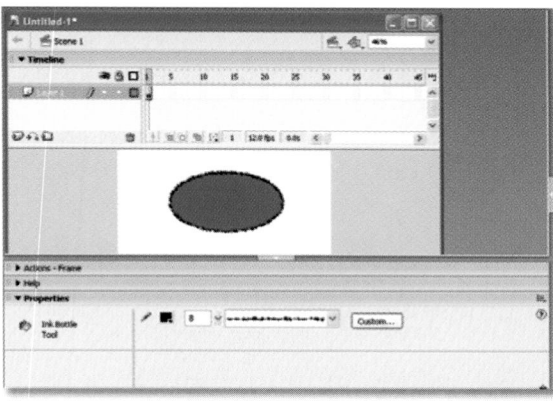

Activate the Ink Bottle Tool, look to the Property inspector, and click the Custom button. Here you'll be able to define your own unique Stroke Style. The variations you can come up with are almost limitless, so feel free to play around and find some you like. I also recommend checking the box that says Zoom 4x to view the style you're creating close up. This customization is not as robust as some custom tools in other programs that you may be used to, but it ain't half bad either.

   HAIRLINE

If you've ever placed any shape that has a stroke into a symbol of any kind and then scaled that symbol by large amounts, you may have noticed some distortion. By default, all your strokes will be one-pixel solid lines. This is great if you have no intention of scaling the shape while in a symbol. It's not so great if you do a lot of scaling and see that the lines are somewhat distorted.

To minimize distortion of outlines, set your stroke to hairline. You can do this when creating the stroke or when using the Ink Bottle Tool, and instead of choosing Solid from the Style drop-down, choose hairline. With this set, you can scale shapes and encounter only minimal distortion, if any, and all your artwork appears a little crisper. Many of you may ask, "Why ever use a one-pixel Solid stroke then?" To tell you the truth, I hardly ever use it. It does appear a bit thicker than hairline, however, so if you want a more noticeable outline, Solid is your man!

SLICK ERASER

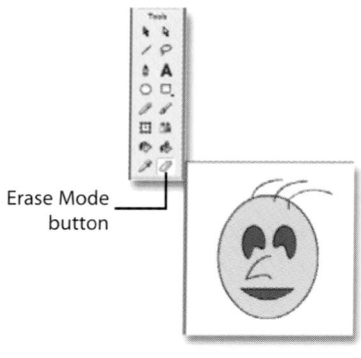

Erase Mode
button

Have you ever finished drawing something and just wished you could go back and erase parts of the stroke or fill but not both at the same time? There are many reasons you may need to do this, but whatever yours is, you'll feel good knowing that it's not only possible but also easy.

Activate the Eraser Tool, click the Eraser Mode option (the one on the left), and select Erase Fills. Now try to erase any shape that has a stroke and a fill and you'll see that the only thing missing when you're done is the area of the fill that you erased. The outline is left untouched. The opposite is true if you select Erase Lines as the mode. Here's a question… Why does Flash refer to strokes as "lines," "strokes," and "outlines" throughout the help system and interface? Interesting. You'll find some other modes here as well that you can play with. They're all fairly self-explanatory; I just wanted to point them out.

   SOMEONE FILL ME UP

Note
small gap

A lot of times I'll use the Pen or Pencil Tool to create some kind of artwork and fill in the colors only after I'm satisfied with my work. This usually means I never fill in the colors. If you work this way or have just an outline and go to fill the shape using the Paint Bucket Tool, only to find that nothing happens, you may be interested in this.

Draw a simple shape (if you don't have one already) with only an outline. Cut a tiny segment out of the outline. Try to fill the shape with the Paint Bucket Tool. Nothing happens, right? Now select the Fill mode option (the button on the left under Options) and choose Close Large Gaps. Try the fill again. Normally a fully-enclosed outline is required for a fill to work, but with this option, you can ignore small gaps in the outline. There's a limit to what Flash will do, but this can be helpful, especially to identify that a tiny gap exists so you can zoom to look for it.

It's an Organizational Hazard

Smooth Working Ahead

If you've read this book straight through without skipping around, then you've no doubt noticed something about my personality. I'm pretty sarcas-

t's an Organizational Hazard

Timeline, Stage, and Library Tips

tic and witty from time to time. My therapist says that I use this to cover my true feelings and that I need to get in touch with my inner child. She called it, "Alone time." The only thing I don't understand is that if it's "alone" time, then why does my inner child have to come along? Personally, I don't think you should force your way into someone else's alone time. It's just rude, which means that my inner child is rude, and that could explain a lot about why I am sarcastic. Once I realized this, I went back to my therapist, told her the story, and said that I felt it would be better if my inner child and I don't talk for a while since he feels the need to disrespect me that way. After about an hour of me explaining the discussion I had with my inner kid, a strange thing happened. My therapist began laughing at us (my child and me). I figured it best if my inner child went to see someone else so there's no conflict of interest, but it's a real pain convincing him to go without me. Okay, so this story has nothing to do with Flash, so you're thinking, "What's the point?" The point is, if you don't read this chapter, you'll go insane.

  NO CAN PAN

This one time, at Pan camp… I learned a little trick to help with certain panning issues. Every now and then, when you're editing a symbol directly without using Edit in Place, you may find that your artwork is so large that you are unable to get the Stage to scroll to view it all. Even if you try to pan to the end, you simply cannot.

Let's just chalk this up to one of those quirky issues in Flash that we love so much. To get around it, you can go to the parent timeline of the symbol you're having trouble with and double-click the instance of the symbol. This will edit that symbol in place, and for some reason, you'll be able to scroll and pan far enough to see the whole thing. Wow, dat's veird!

   THE RIGID GRID

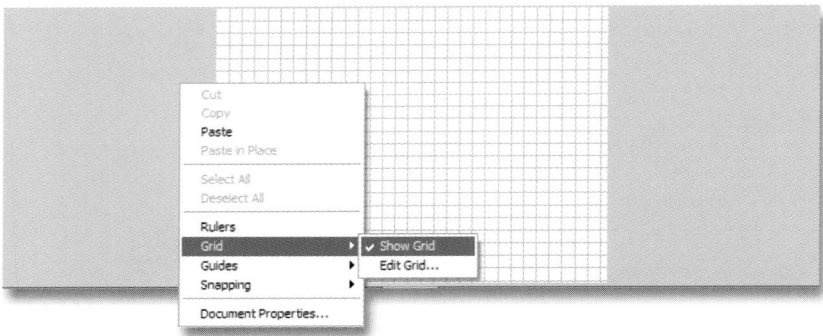

Every time I use Flash, I find that I want to align my symbols, objects, shapes, and text perfectly with as little work as possible. What can I say, I'm a little lazy. To help with that, there is an option in Flash that enables you to view a layout grid on your Stage. Either right-click your Stage and go to Grid > Show Grid, or if you want to be really fast, use CTRL-' on your keyboard.

Look at that! Now you can make sure that all your objects are aligned the way you want them at all times without having to use the Align panel. Oh, did I mention that you can edit the Grid properties by selecting Edit Grid instead of Show Grid? Well, now I have. You can change spacing or color, enable snapping to grid lines, and change the accuracy of snapping, allowing you to be as lazy as you want to be. And it's okay to export while grids are on, because they will not appear in your final movie.

UNDERSCORE MY RISE TO THE TOP

A document's Library can contain a number of different objects, from folders and video to movie clips and buttons. Normally the items in the Library are ordered alphabetically from A to Z. If you have a ton of folders in your Library as well, you'll notice that they're scattered around in the item list in alphabetical order, too. Because most of us are used to folders being anchored to the top of a list (like in Windows/Mac operating systems), why don't we do the same thing in our Library?

By putting an underscore "_" in front of the folder name, you can anchor that folder to the top of the Library. Doing this to all your folders will put them all at the top and alphabetize your folders separately from the rest of your assets. Whew, that looks a lot better.

CHANGING FRAMES

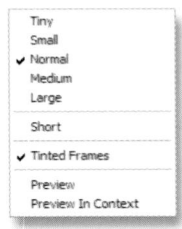

Although the Flash Timeline can appear to be quite static and boring, there are actually some very interesting options that can make your Timeline much more useful. At the top-right corner of the Timeline, you'll see a mini timeline button. Clicking it will give you various frame view options. You can set how wide Flash displays the frames or even make them vertically compact by choosing Short. If tinted frame sequences get on your nerves for some reason, turn them off. And the most fun are the last two on the list. Choosing either of the Preview options will let you actually see a scaled-down icon of the objects in your frames, sort of like a preview. Of course these are all view options, so they have no effect on how the frames operate, but they could help you see the frames the way that's best for you. Whoever said the Flash Timeline was boring?

THAT'S SOME FINE MOVEMENT

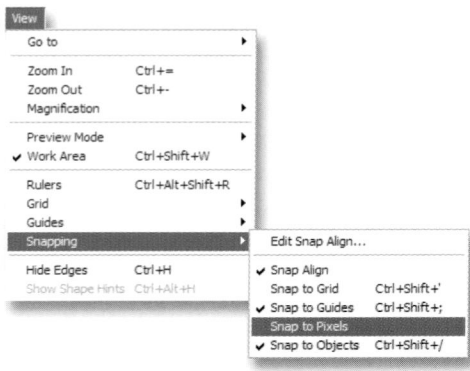

Normally when you zoom in or out, the number of pixels a selected object will move when you nudge it with arrow keys changes based on the zoom factor. If you'd like to make sure that your objects move only 1 pixel at a time, regardless of the magnification of your view, you can enable Snap to Pixels by going under View, then Snapping and choosing Snap to Pixels. Another cool thing is that when you're zoomed to 400% or more, you'll see a nifty pixel grid to which all objects will be constrained. To temporarily disable or enable (depends on current state) the pixel grid and pixel snapping, press the X key. When you release it, the grid and snapping will return to the set state.

SYMBOLIC JUMPING

If you have many symbols in many directories of your Library, finding the right one to edit can be a bit time-consuming. Try this really quick way to find and edit a symbol in your Library. Look to the top right of the Stage window where you'll see an icon with shapes on it that is just to the left of the View Magnification drop-down. Clicking this Edit Symbols icon will give you a drop-down menu of every folder and symbol in your Library. Clicking on any one will take you to its timeline for editing. It's much faster than hunting through the tree structure of the Library. The only drawback is that this only works for symbols, not bitmaps, fonts, and other things that may also be in a Library. Incidentally, the icon just to the left of the Edit Symbols will do the same for scenes in your document. Things couldn't be much faster than that.

THE NUDGE FACTOR

Any time you select an object on the Stage in Flash and move it around using your arrow keys, you'll move the item a varying number of pixels based on your view scale. Here's how it works. If you are at 100%, a simple arrow key nudge will move the item 1 pixel in that direction. Holding down the SHIFT key while nudging will move it 10 times as far (10 pixels). If you set your view scale to 50%, a nudge will move it 2 pixels and a SHIFT nudge will be 20 pixels. The opposite is true when your view scale is set to 200%. You can use this information to figure out how far Flash will move your selected objects. But as you can see, if you set your view to some arbitrary number like 34%, you'll have a much harder time determining the nudge factor.

Here's a formula you can use to figure out those complex ones. For regular nudge, use 1/(Zoom Percentage/100). For SHIFT nudge, use 10/(Zoom Percentage/100).

MULTIPLE SELECT IN THE LIBRARY

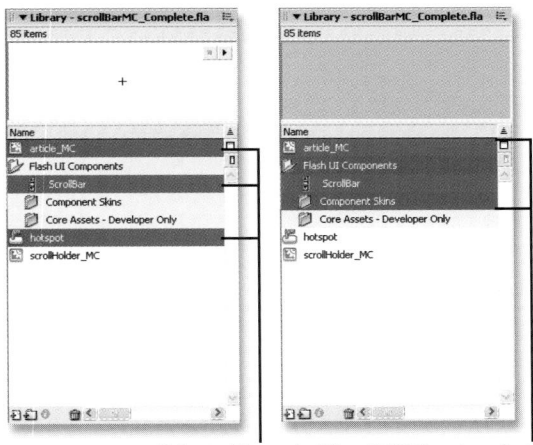

Selected items holding SHIFT key to select a sequential group of items at once

If you have determined that several items in your Library that are currently scattered all over need to be put in a folder or deleted from the Library, there's an easy way. At first you might approach the issue by picking each one and pressing the trash can at the bottom right of the Library to remove it. Well, repeating these two steps over and over for each item could take forever.

Instead, select all the items at once by holding down the CTRL key (CMD on Mac) as you select each item. Once you have them all selected, you can either drag them wherever you want, or, to remove them, just click the trash can once. The same concept works items in the Stage and Timeline, but you must use SHIFT instead of CTRL. Think of it as one of the little games Flash plays with our minds.

   FOLDERS NEST TOO

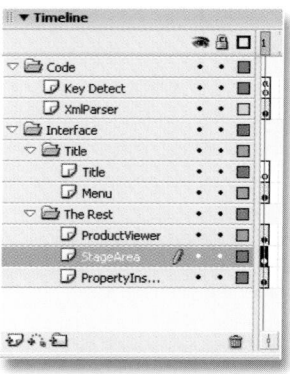

Flash documents are getting more and more complex as features are added. As a result, you often end up with timelines that have several layers on them. Organizing these layers becomes more difficult, and sometimes simply naming them doesn't do enough for that organization. One feature that aids in organizing a timeline is Layer Folders. And because folders also can start cluttering up a timeline pretty quickly, we must go even further to prevent our timelines from looking like a musical score sheet. To do this, we turn to nesting. That's right, we can actually nest folders in the Timeline as well. To do so, simply create a Layer Folder using the Add Folder button a couple of times. With several folders on the Timeline, you can click and drag one into another, and of course the same still goes for layers themselves. By nesting your layers, you'll save screen space and keep your layers well organized from this day forward.

   SYMBOLISM

Have you ever wondered what symbols are for? Do you read chapter after chapter in other Flash books and feel they overcomplicate things? Then this one may be for you. The basic rule for converting a shape into a symbol is that you should make a symbol when you are going to reuse any object or shape over and over. So if you have anything on your Stage that you use multiple times, then turn it into a symbol. Then you can place instances of the symbol on your Stage that point back to the original by dragging the symbol from the Library onto your Stage. So there's the basic rule. Of course there are many more reasons to use them, but if you want to delve into all that, then read a book that has the complicated explanations. You won't hurt my feelings, I promise. Well, maybe a little.

  LET ME SEE YOUR MASK

Previewing your nested mask effects can be time-consuming if you have to make tiny adjustments without the advantage of a real time preview. You end up going back and forth each time you make a change. That's why Flash allows you to preview your mask effect in the authoring environment. To do so, set up a mask as normal and then simply lock all the layers included in your mask. You must lock the mask layer as well as all masked layers for the preview to work correctly. After the layers are locked, you can preview the effect by playing or scrubbing through your Timeline as usual. The only difference is that now you can see your mask and how it looks without using Test Movie or Publish. Even though this function should work quite well, remember that there is no substitute for actually testing or publishing your movie. For instance, using the authoring preview will not properly show masking for embedded fonts and therefore should be used only as a time-saving guide.

THE GUIDING LINE

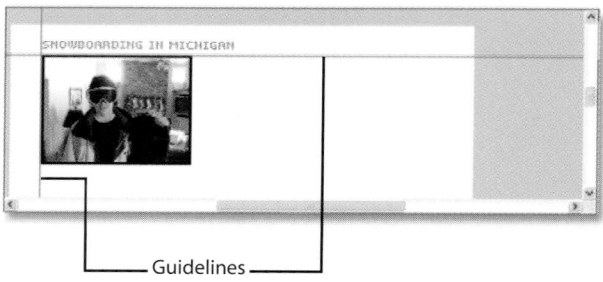

Guidelines

Aligning artwork, text, and other objects on your Stage can be a useful capability. Let's say you have to make sure that all your text on the Stage is divided evenly into three columns. Because Flash doesn't support tables of any kind, this could be tricky.

When rulers are turned on in Flash (View > Rulers or CTRL-ALT-SHIFT-R; OPT-SHIFT-CMD-R on Mac), you can create a guide to help you align and organize your artwork. To create a guide, click a ruler and drag onto your stage. You can make both vertical and horizontal guides to lend a hand, and the best part is that they are not part of your exported SWF movie. They're just there to help and nothing more. Isn't that sweet?

These guys don't respond to CTRL-Z (Undo), so to remove a guide line, drag it back onto the ruler from whence it came, and it disappears.

INVISIBLE LAYER

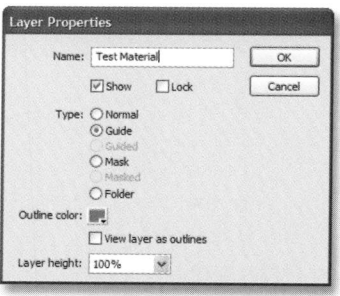

All layers in Flash are not created equal. I'm sure you're aware or have at least seen the different layer types Flash can create. For the most part, any layer you create will export the items on it to your final SWF movie. This is not true for guide layers. Add some artwork to your stage on a particular layer and change the layer to a guide by double-clicking the layer and selecting Guide. Now test the movie (CTRL-ENTER), and you'll see that nothing on your guide layer is actually visible.

This can come in handy when you want to see what your movie will look like without certain items, without having to actually delete them. If you ever use Templates, you'll see that the instructions are on a guide layer so they don't interfere with the project. If there are items you want to permanently remove, do not rely on this tip because while a guide is invisible, the overall file size of the document is still affected by artwork on one.

 REVERSAL

Have you ever had a section of animation on your Timeline that you really liked, but there was just one little problem—it goes the wrong way? There's a nifty little tool that you can use to actually take a selected set of frames and reverse them with a few easy steps.

Select the series of frames in the Timeline that you want to reverse, right-click (CTRL-click on Mac) the selection, and choose Reverse Frames from the list. Flash will do its best to reverse the animation in the Timeline. The outcome will be just as though you were actually playing the original backwards. This can cause some strange effects sometimes, so keep your hand over the Undo button just in case. However, if you make sure that your selection starts and ends with a keyframe, chances are it will turn out pretty darn good.

 STRETCH THOSE FRAMES

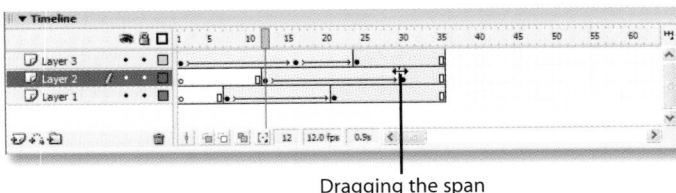

Dragging the span

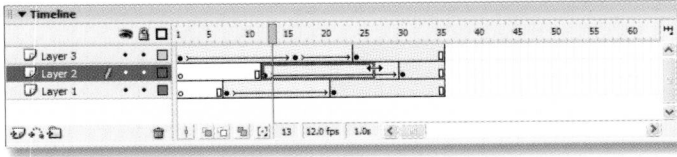

There is a quicker way to move a keyframe than having to select it, release, and then click the highlighted keyframe and drag again. That's the typical way you would move any keyframe or frame for that matter in Flash's Timeline. Instead, roll over any keyframe in your Timeline while holding down CTRL (OPT on Mac) and you'll notice your cursor changes to a double-headed arrow. Hovering slightly to the left of the keyframe will grab the end of the frame span to the left of it, while hovering to the right will affect the beginning of that span. Click and drag while over either side to adjust the frame spans without going through the hassle of the normal method for moving frames.

CHAPTER 3 · Timeline, Stage, and Library Tips   **45**

  ## HERE'S AN OUTLINE

Flash actually gives you the ability to render all art-work on any layer as outlines only. Choose any layer in your Timeline with artwork on it and click the colored square to the right of that layer's name. Flash will display everything on that layer as out-lines in the color of the square icon.

There are a number of reasons to use the feature: You may want to determine what artwork goes on what layer simply by looking and matching the outline color. You may want to position an object under another without the fill color getting in the way. Whatever the case, you now know the solu-tion. Some things you should know: Outlines only appear in Flash, not when you export the movie, and rendering art in outline mode can speed up Flash on slower machines. Click the same icon again to return the layer's view mode to normal.

   ## LIBRARY PREVIEW

Play button

Before choosing an animating symbol to place on your Stage, why not take a peek at what it will look like? Select any symbol in your Library that has more than one frame on its Timeline (graphic, movie clip, or button), and if the symbol has animation in it, the preview at the top of the Library will display a miniature play and stop button for you. Pressing the play button will play a tiny preview of the animation in that symbol once.

I often use this preview when I plain forget what a symbol has in it. I'd much rather see a tiny quick preview than have to go to the Timeline to see what's up.

This works for imported sounds as well, but I'm sorry to say that it doesn't work for imported video. So don't freak out when you select a video clip and there's no playback control in the preview area. That's just the way it is.

  ## ORDER IN THE LAYER!

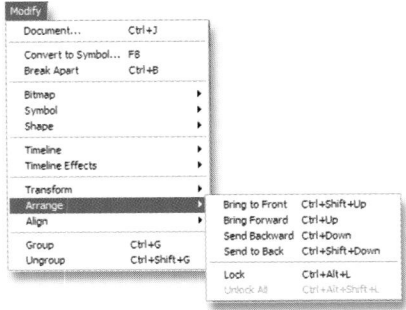

So you've figured out that moving a layer on top of another layer will ensure that all the objects on that layer will always be on top of any objects under it. There is another way to fiddle with what's on top of what, but not many people talk about it.

On a layer with multiple objects, select an object, go to Modify, then Arrange, and then choose Bring to Front. Now move any other object on the same layer so it overlaps with that object, and you'll see that it falls underneath it. Now you can use Send to Back on the same object and see it covered by any other object on that layer. Using Bring Forward/Back will advance or retreat it one level, relative to the other objects in the same layer. It's kinda like layers within layers.

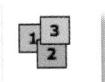

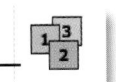

After selecting
3 and pressing
Send to Back —

Keep in mind that an arrangement only applies to objects of the same layer, and none of this applies to shapes. Shapes always appear under any object on a layer and their arrangement cannot be altered.

   ## ALL LAYERS... ATTENTION!

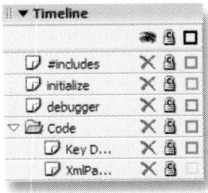

Each layer in a Timeline has three quick settings that you can apply with a click—Show/Hide, Lock/Unlock, and Outlines/Normal. Each one has an icon at the top of its column telling you what it does. The only thing you may not be aware of is that those three icons are clickable as well. Clicking on any of them will toggle that option for every layer at once.

Try clicking the eye icon to hide all the layers in the Timeline at once and you'll see what I mean. A good way to make use of these icons would be to quickly lock all your layers and then unlock only the one you want to work on. Use 'em however you want, but don't forget that these guys are there.

  DUPLICATES FOR SAFETY

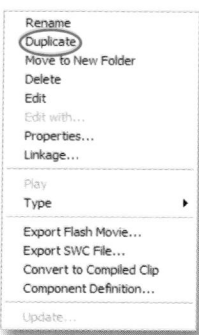

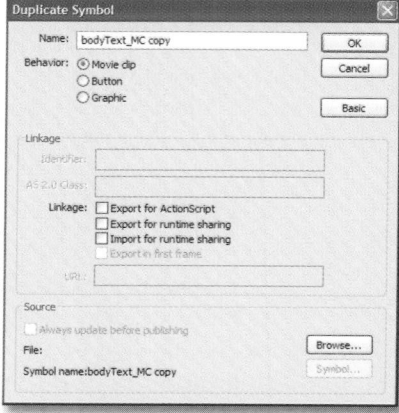

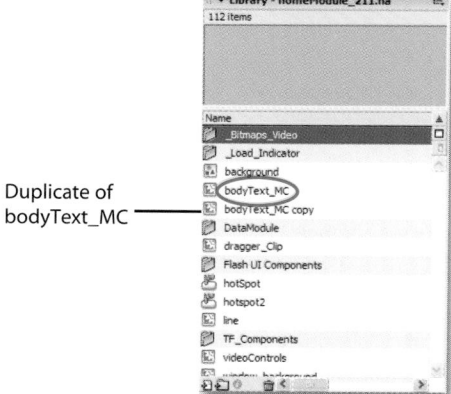

Duplicate of
bodyText_MC

I've worked with Flash for several years now, and the most important lesson I ever learned was to back up your work. You may have noticed that this book has several tips on how to do this effectively. That's because I learned the hard way over and over again. I shed a lot of tears so that you would not have to.

If you want to make changes to any symbol in your Library and want to make sure that you can revert back if things go wrong, do this….

Right-click on the symbol you want to change and choose Duplicate. Give it any name you like and make your changes to the original. Now you have a copy that you can always go back to if your changes don't work out. Another advantage is that you don't have to save a new file to safely make minor changes to one symbol (although I do recommend doing that from time to time as well).

  ## SMALLER PREVIEW

One of the most feature-rich panels in Flash is not really a panel at all. It's more of a window, and it's called the Library. Perhaps you've heard of it? The preview window at the top of the Library is probably one of the coolest things about it, but I have to be honest. I don't really use this thing all that much. I know I should, and so should you, but I guess I've just fallen into some poor habits. Either way, if it goes unused, you can prevent it from taking up so much space by dragging the bar that separates the preview area from the asset list all the way to the top. It won't fully disappear, but it will certainly be out of your way. Hey look, aren't those little tiny previews cute?

Drag this up to shrink preview area

 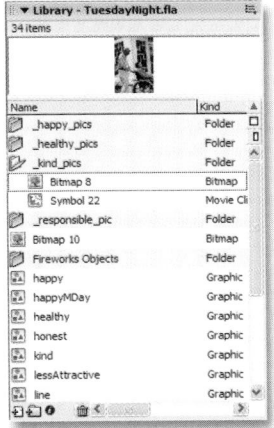

  ## FRAMES OF A LAYER FLOCK TOGETHER

Click the icon to select all frames for a layer

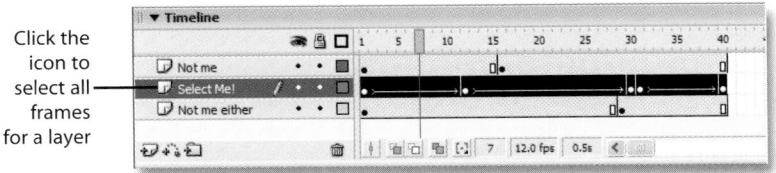

Selecting all the frames for a single layer is something I do a lot. Given the fact that you can have thousands of frames on a layer, dragging your mouse to select them all may not be the best way. So don't do it that way. Instead, simply click any layer's icon to immediately select all its frames. Wow, this advanced Flash work is making me tired. I think I'm going to have a nap.

SAME BACKGROUND, DIFFERENT SCENE

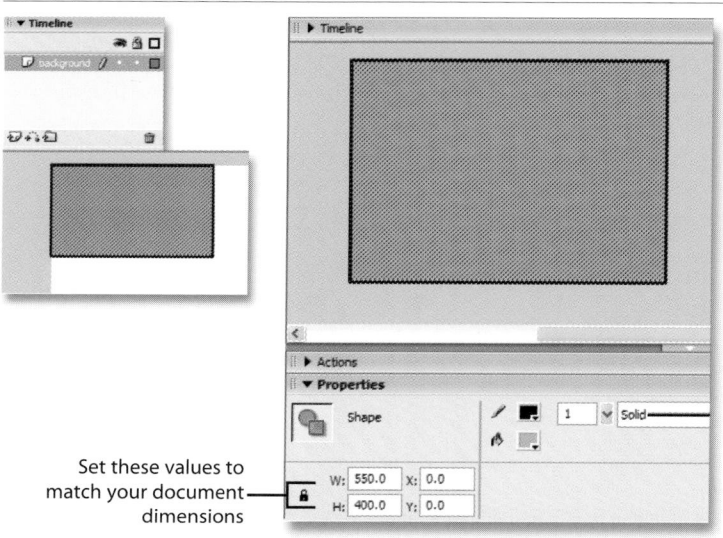

Set these values to match your document dimensions

If you're big into scenes, I'm sure you've noticed that once you set the background color for your document, every scene has the same one. This is because the document background covers every bit of the document, and there's nothing you can do to change that.

There is a trick though. Create a new layer and name it "background." Draw a rectangle on the layer and resize it using the Property inspector so that it's the exact size of your document. Set its position to 0,0, make sure the layer is under all others, and lock it. You end up with a background layer that can be placed in different scenes and changed to whatever color you like for each. Vóila! Custom backgrounds on any timeline or scene in your document.

You could even go the extra mile and make symbols for each background color to use and change the original symbol to alter many backgrounds at once. Hey, that's kinda like style-sheets for HTML.

ADD FRAMES TO ALL LAYERS

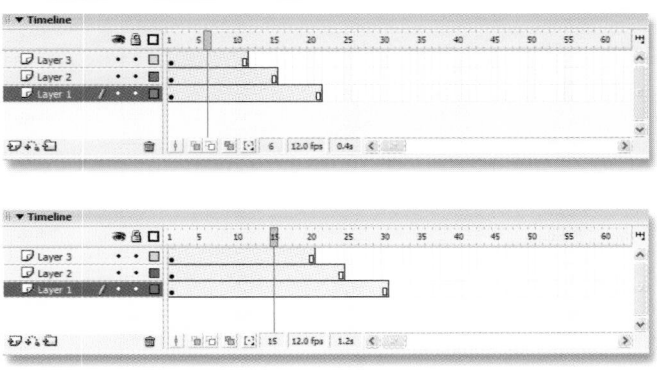

To quickly extend your animation, you already know to use F5 (Insert Frame). Normally, you select a frame on the Timeline on the layer you wish to extend and then press F5 until satisfied. If you have several layers, you may want to save yourself some time by not having to repeat the process for every layer.

Move the Timeline marker (the red line) to a certain area of your Timeline where you want to add frames for all layers and press ESC to unselect any selected frames. Now, pressing F5 will add frames for every layer on the Timeline at that location. Let's just say that this can save a lot of time if you have thirty or forty layers like I've seen in some people's Timelines.

THE LIBRARY TELLS ALL

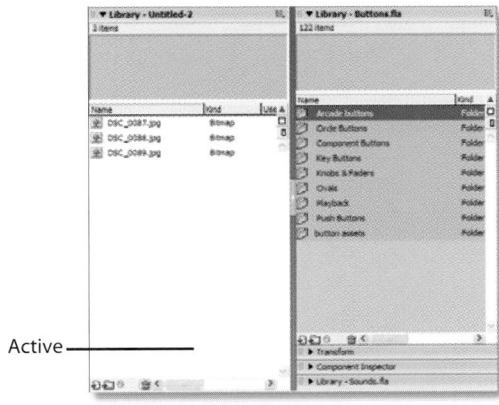

Active

When you're working on several open files at the same time, it can be hard to tell what document you're currently viewing. Trust me, there have been many times that I made changes to a timeline and realized I was working in the wrong file. Sure, part of it is me not paying attention…all of it actually, but still. The Library can help you with this if you have it open. The background color of the Library is usually white, but when you have more than one of them open at a time, the inactive ones have gray backgrounds.

This can help you determine what file you're working in with just a glance. I know it seems trivial, but it's saved me many times.

  I MISS FLASH 5

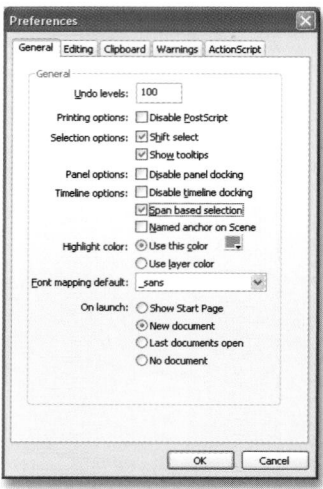

I don't think too many people actually miss Flash 5 as a whole, but it did have one quality that people talk about to this day. That would be the span-based selection in the Timeline. For those of you who never saw it, it does have its benefits, although it takes some getting used to. Either way, if you want it back, all you have to do is pay a visit to your preferences window (CTRL-U or Flash > Preferences on Mac) and put a check by Span based selection.

This will allow you to select a sequence of frames from one keyframe to the next in your Timeline by simply clicking any frame in between. You can also grab the end of a frame sequence and drag all at once to resize that sequence. If this helps you in your work, then never fear: Macromedia has listened carefully and kept the Flash 5 span-based Timeline around as an option.

   HARVEST THE ASSETS

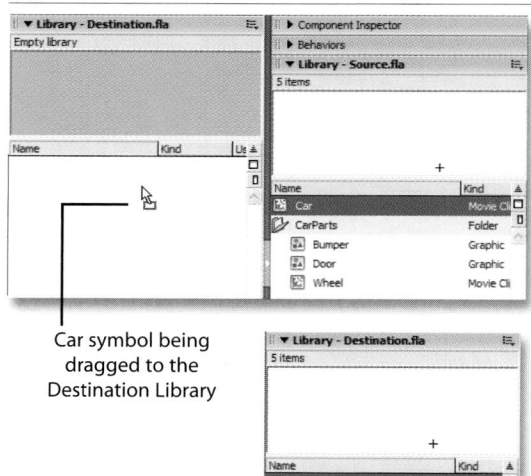

Car symbol being dragged to the Destination Library

Let's say you have two separate documents, and each one has assets in its Library that you'd like in the other. Open both files at the same time and open both of their Libraries. Getting an item from one document to the other is as easy as dragging that asset from one Library to the next. Let's say you have a car symbol that contains the symbols tire, door, and bumper. Dragging the car symbol to another Library will automatically copy the other assets it uses along with it. Flash is pretty clever sometimes.

WHAT'S WITH THE WARNING?

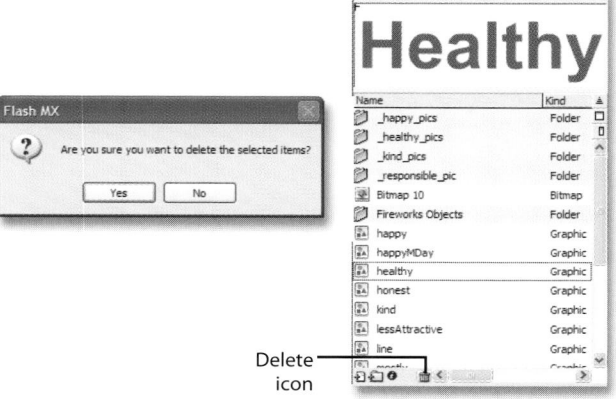

Delete
icon

Removing items from the Library is certainly something you need to do carefully, but Flash pops up a warning when you do that makes it seem as though it's an action that you can't take back. This is not the case. If you ever remove something from your Library and immediately decide that you miss it and want it back, press CTRL-Z. It'll be just like the whole thing never happened. Now if they'd only add an undo for formatting your hard drive, I'd be all set.

   **GET READY TO SCRUB IN**

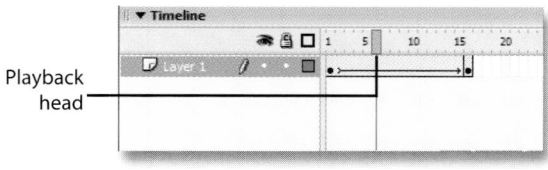

Playback
head

If you don't have a wheel button on your mouse or are working on a Mac, then you can skip this one. Using the Flash Timeline well is a very important skill, and many people get frustrated and give up. Hey, more work for the rest of us. And because you've decided to stay in the game (and buy my book), I'm going to give you a nice little tip for how to move through the Timeline with the greatest of ease. Moving through the Timeline is called *scrubbing* and typically it's done in several slow and clunky ways, some of which I've already outlined in this very book. There is one method that is simply the fastest of them all. Good luck on your journey to find that way.

No, I would never do that to you. Activate your stage in any Flash document by clicking anywhere on it. Now hold down the SHIFT key and scroll your mouse wheel. Scrolling up will move your playback head forward in the Timeline, while scrolling the wheel down moves the head backward. Oh, and one more thing—holding down the CTRL key while using the mouse wheel will jump you to the beginning and end of the Timeline.

Win Lose or Draw? Draw!

Animation Avenue

Whenever people ask me what Flash is used for, I say, "I have no idea—I just pay some guy to do all my work and copy things I read in other books." They

Win, Lose, or Draw? Draw!
Create Better Effects and Animations

usually look at me for a second and then begin to cry. I can't explain it, but maybe it's because around that time I kick them in the shin. So finally I had to ask someone what Flash's purpose is and here's what they said… "Well, Shane, Flash is first and foremost an animation tool. When it was first used, the sole purpose was to allow for compact, fluid animations that were small in size and nice to look at. The interesting thing is that with the onset of the post-war ethical… blah, blah, blah." That's about the time I phased out of the conversation. What I did learn is that Flash is capable of creating very powerful animations, so I decided to dedicate this chapter to teaching all of you the secrets of making your animations faster, prettier, and better.

   CUSTOM GRADIENTS

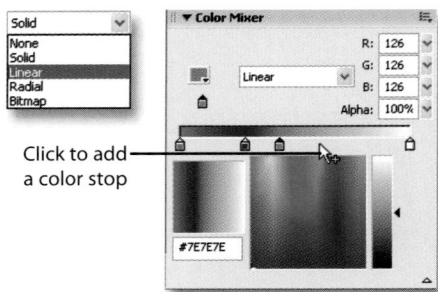

Click to add a color stop

Let's face it, the default gradients in Flash are pretty much worthless. I'm sure they had their reasons for including these particular gradients, but I can't fathom what they are. Thank God we are able to make our own. To do so, go to the Color Mixer panel (open it using SHIFT-F9) and choose Linear or Radial instead of Solid from the drop-down menu. To edit an existing color, select the little square handle under the Gradient bar (known as a *color stop*) and choose a new color from the spectrum. To add a new Color stop, click anywhere along the gradient bar where you see your cursor has a little plus sign next to it. To remove a stop, click it and drag down until you see it disappear. When you have a gradient that you are happy with, click the Color Mixer's panel menu (top right) and choose Add Swatch. You'll now see your new gradient listed along with the other defaults. Custom swatches are visible only for the file you make them in.

  REALISTIC SPHERE

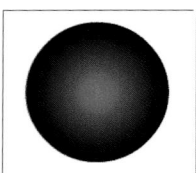

We all know that Flash doesn't support true 3D objects. So how do people make those shapes that appear to be 3D? For example, it would be nice to make a somewhat realistic-looking sphere, don't you think? Let's try it. Draw a basic circle with no stroke and a simple spherical gradient from the default list of gradients in the color picker. Activate the Fill Transform Tool from the Toolbar and select the circle on your Stage. You'll see that you now have four handles that appear, each controlling a different aspect of the gradient. First grab the circle in the center of the gradient and drag it slightly up and to the left. Now grab

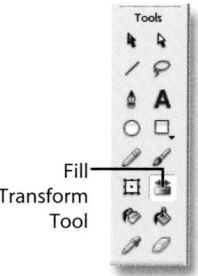

Fill Transform Tool

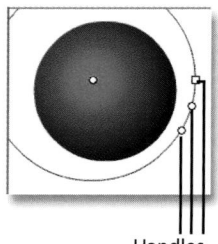

the middle handle of the right three and drag it down and to the left so that the gradient appears as though it's a 3D light cast down on a real sphere. You may need to adjust here and there to get the right effect, and turning off Snap To Objects can help your dragging accuracy. Hey, not a bad-looking sphere!

Handles

AM I TRIPPING?

For some, this will be useful; for others, just a fun, trippy thing to do every once in a while to impress your friends. When you have any tween or any movement on your Timeline by any means, there is an option in the Flash Timeline to let you view several frames of an animation at a time. This feature is referred to as Onion Skinning, but without the tears. To enable Onion Skinning, look to the bottom of the Timeline directly under the first frame. The second button from the left toggles the Onion Skinning mode.

Once you're in that mode, you can move the black brackets above the Timeline by grabbing their center to cover the desired range you want to be included in the Onion Skinning view. This can be very useful when applying frame-by-frame animation techniques because it enables you to see ahead or behind for a reference.

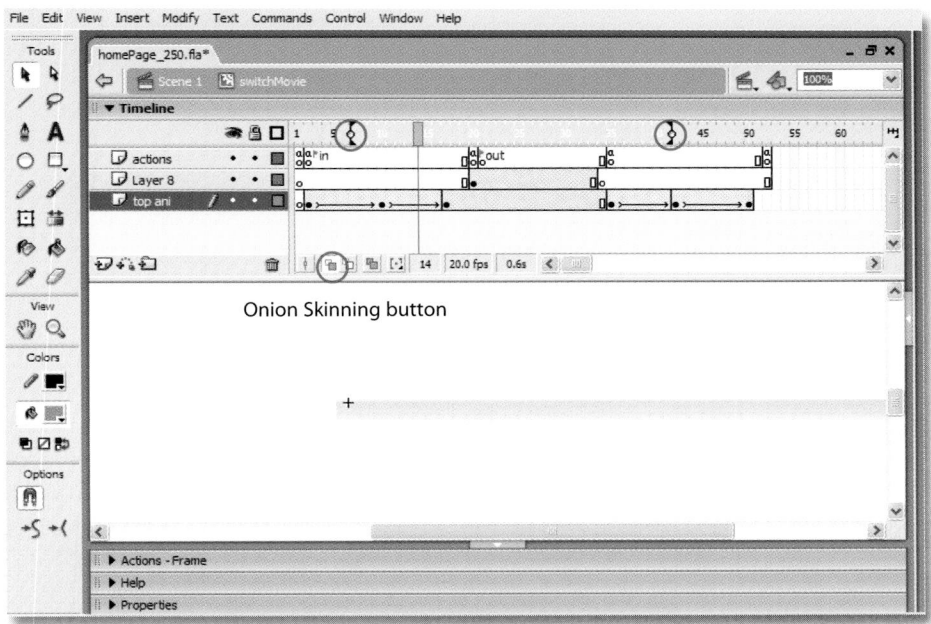

Onion Skinning button

REALISTIC DROP-SHADOW

With Flash MX 2004, you get built-in set of Timeline Effects and one of them even allows you to create a drop-shadow for any object. The only problem is that the result looks very amateurish. Why not make a more realistic drop-shadow? Start by drawing a simple circle on your Stage. Now select it, copy it using CTRL-C, create a new Layer, and name it "shadow." With the shadow layer selected, press CTRL-SHIFT-V (Paste in Place). This will paste the circle in the exact same position as where you copied it from, but of course on your new layer. Now move that newly pasted circle a few pixels to the right and down so that it goes slightly beyond the original. Next, change the color of the shadow circle to any shade of gray using the Paint Bucket. With the gray circle selected, go

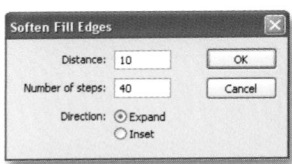 

under Modify, then Shape, then choose Soften Fill Edges. Enter 10 for the distance and 40 for the number of steps and then click OK. Finally, move the shadow layer beneath the original layer in the Timeline. The end result is a pretty nice-looking drop-shadow effect, and of course you could follow the same steps for any shape you may have.

   ### CAREFUL WITH THOSE SHAPES

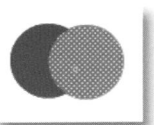

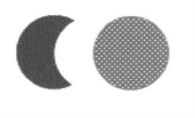

Flash is very unique in the way it handles shapes that overlap each other. For this to work, the shapes mentioned must be on the same layer. Create a blue circle and a red circle on your Stage. Now overlap the red circle with the blue. Now unselect the blue circle by pressing ESC and then move the blue circle away from the red. You'll notice that the blue circle has taken a bite out of the red. Basically, in Flash, if you overlap shapes of different colors, they cut into each other; whereas, shapes of the same color will actually combine to form a unified shape. Many have argued over the usefulness of this behavior, but imagine trying to create a perfect half moon without this ability. Sure it's possible, but after how much work? I for one think this behavior allows for limitless uses that you can now go out and discover. Go my children, explore.

   LOOK MA, THEY'RE PERFECT

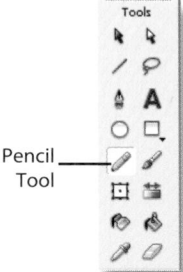

Pencil Tool

Ever wondered how Da Vinci drew that perfect circle? He used Flash, of course. Select the Pencil Tool from the Toolbar and make sure to set the Pencil Mode under Options to Straighten. I know, it sounds strange to use Straighten when you want to draw a perfect circle, but trust me on this one. Now draw the best circle you can on your Stage. If you get even marginally close, Flash will make it perfect for you. Now you can try drawing other shapes like ovals, rectangles, and triangles and watch Flash continue to make perfect shapes for you. Of course, Flash can only do so

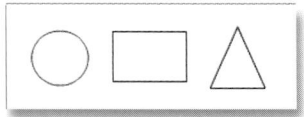

much, so don't think that drawing some whacked-out circle will result in one that Da Vinci himself would envy. Flash simply does the best it can, so you have to get kinda close.

   QUICK, PUT ON THE MASK!

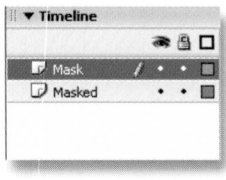

For a simple Mask effect in a few short steps, start by placing some artwork to be the mask on a layer. Now create a new layer and put all your items to be masked on that layer. It is wise to name the layers, so you might as well name them "Mask" and "Masked" respectively. Now comes the hard part. Move the Mask layer so that it is directly above the layer containing the items to be masked. Now double-click the Mask layer, set its type to Mask, and click OK. Flash should automatically include the layer under the Mask layer as being masked and lock both layers for you, which enables you to preview the Mask effect.

If for some reason Flash does not automatically do this (it has its issues), then double-click the Masked layer, set it to Masked, and then lock both layers. That was pretty dern easy now, wadn't it? Yeehaw!

   PREBUILT ANIMATIONS

There are a lot of Flash programs out there that have built-in animations and are designed solely to let people animate things without needing to really know how a Flash Timeline

works. Well, guess what? Go ahead, guess. Okay, I'll tell you. Flash now has its own built-in Animations, referred to as Timeline Effects. It's as simple as can be to apply one. Right-click on any object (shape, symbol, and so on) on your Stage and go to Timeline Effects, which will display a list of pre-built effects for you to choose from. Picking any effect will usually bring up a quick little settings window that enables you to specify parameters for the effect. Once you think you have what you want, click OK and Flash does all the work for you. After an effect has been applied, you can easily change it or remove it by selecting Edit or Remove Effect from the same place you picked the effect itself, after right-clicking the object with the effect applied, of course.

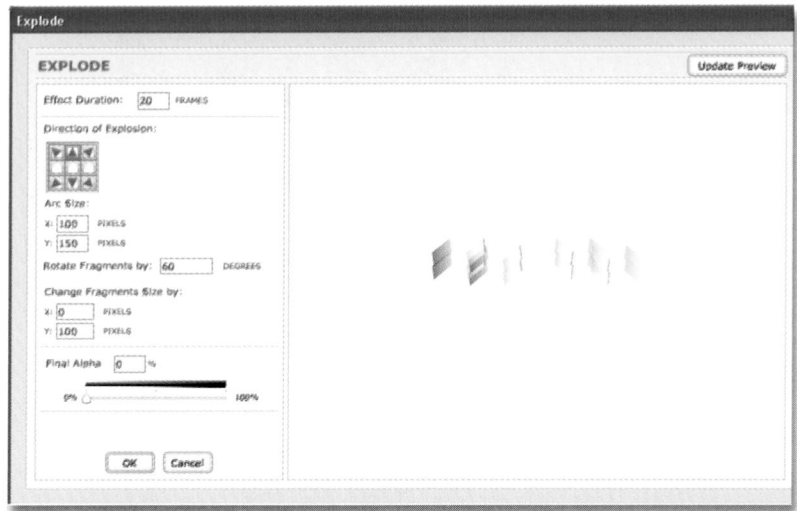

GUIDING A MASK OR MASKING A GUIDE

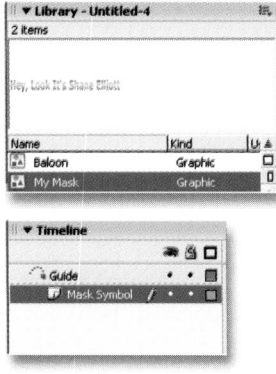

Although creating Motion Guides and Masks can be relatively straightforward, what may not be is how to combine the two effects. Let's say you want to apply a mask to some objects that are part of a Motion Guide. At first you may consider moving your guided layers under your Mask layer, but that will just disable one or the other and make your guided layers masked. Instead, try placing your Mask effect in a movie clip that you create in your Library. Put only your mask and masked layers in the movie clip, and when you have it just the way you want it, you can switch to the Timeline where the guide is or create a guide if one does not exist. Now place your newly created symbol containing your Mask effect on a layer under your guide, attach it to the guide path, set that layer to be guided, and vóila!

You can now effectively guide a mask. Of course, the same process works in the other direction when masking a guide, but it can require some more time to make sure that your guided animation is fully visible through the area you defined as your mask.

   TEXT THAT MORPHS

You can use a Shape Tween when you want to move a shape across the Stage or to change a circle into a square. However, you can't apply a Shape Tween to text fields and have them morph from one word to another. Can you? Actually you can, but there are a few steps involved in doing so. As you may or may not know, a text field is not a shape, it's an object, and objects respond to Motion Tweens, not Shape Tweens, so it's time to be clever.

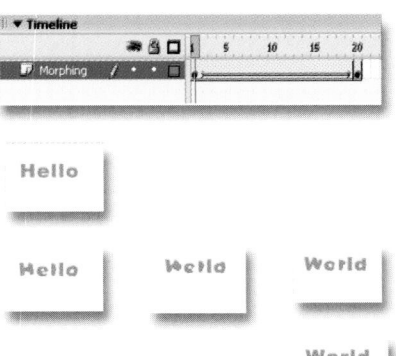

Add some text to the first frame of your Timeline. Now add a keyframe to frame 20 and change the text there to something different from what's on frame 1. Now (with the text field selected) press CTRL-B to Break Apart the text field. At first it will separate the word into individual letter blocks. Press CTRL-B again to break those letters into shapes. Repeat that step for the text on frame 1.

Finally create a Shape Tween to animate between the two keyframes. There it is, a neat little text effect commonly referred to as *morphing*.

   STRETCH IT TO THE LIMIT

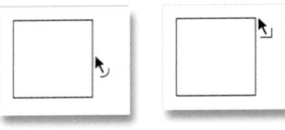

What happens when you drag a line segment

What happens when you drag a corner point

There are several applications that are designed to create vector artwork—Flash included, of course. The ways in which these programs enable you to create that artwork, however, is not always the same. Case in point would be the capability in Flash to manipulate shapes you've drawn. Start by drawing a simple circle or square and then activate the Arrow Tool (V). Roll over the edge of the shape you drew until you see a small curved line beside your arrow cursor. Click and drag in any direction. When you let go, you'll see that your once-simple shape is now quite custom. Grabbing points as opposed to a straight area will produce different results.

This ability to manipulate shapes with such ease is a key benefit to using Flash, so I suggest you exploit it. There is just no limit to what you can do, so stretch it to the limit one more time!

  REALISTIC MOTION

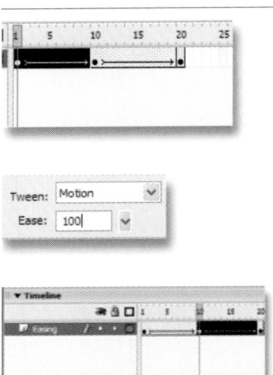

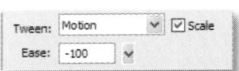

One of the hardest things to do in animation is recreate a realistic movement that you might see in real life. Create a circle, convert it to a symbol, and then create a quick animation using a Motion Tween so that the circle moves up and then back down to its original position (similar to the motion of a ball bouncing). Select any frame in the first Motion Tween, go to the Property inspector, and set the numeric Ease value to 100. Now select any frame in the second Motion Tween and set its Ease value to -100. Play your animation again and you will see that the animation looks very much like a real ball being thrown up into the air.

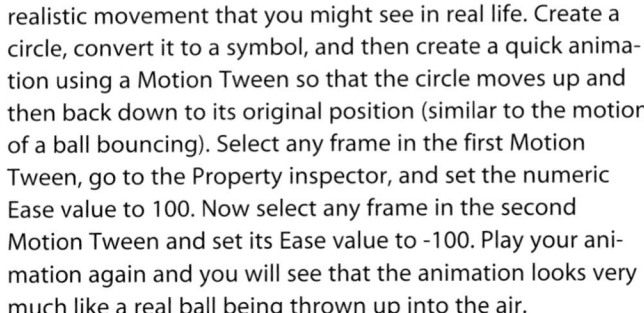

Any negative number is for easing in, meaning the animation will begin slow and speed up, while a positive value means the opposite. You can also use the slider to change the Ease value instead of typing it in.

SIMPLIFY YOUR SHAPES

Often, whether you draw a shape by hand in Flash or import vector artwork from another application such as Illustrator or Freehand, there is a similar result—a result that we are often unaware of. Shapes can become overly complex with irregular curves or crooked lines. To simplify these shapes, Flash gives you two options. Click the Arrow Tool and look at the two options at the base of the Toolbar. On the left, you see Smooth, and on the right, Straighten. Both of these options can help to simplify the number of points in your shapes, thereby making the shapes faster to render and reducing your file size a little. To apply either of these effects, simply select a shape, activate your Arrow Tool, and press either button. This will apply the simplification and slightly change the look of your drawing. Oh, and you can apply these multiple times to optimize the shape more and more each time.

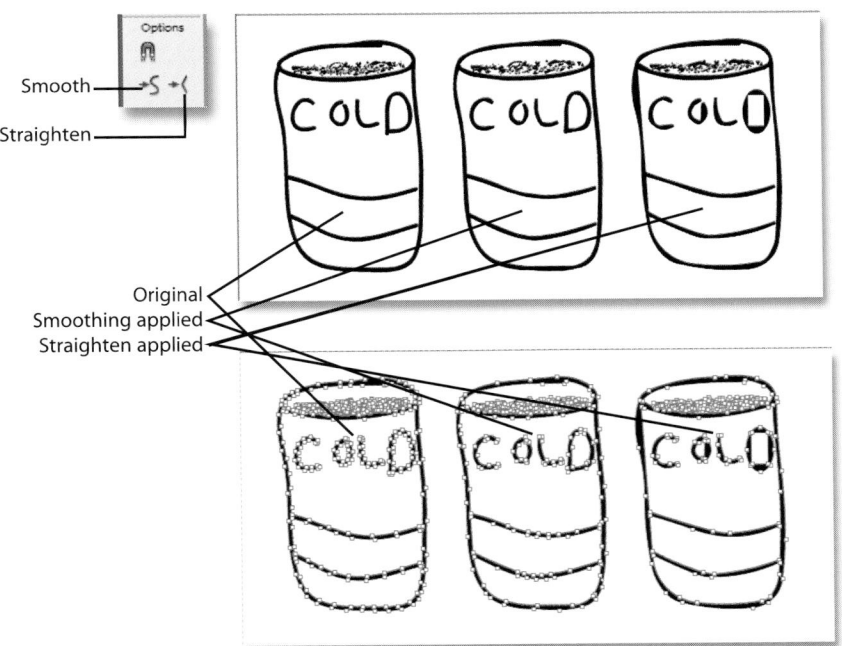

   CUSTOM EASING

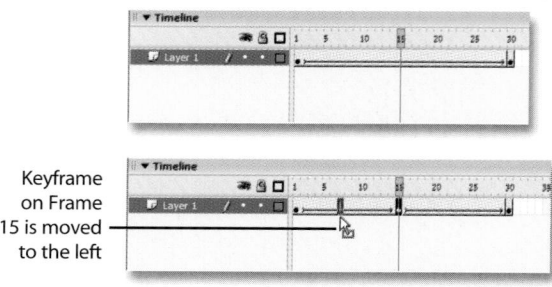

Keyframe on Frame 15 is moved to the left

Setting the Ease value of a tween in the Property inspector is very effective for making some more interesting animations. There is another way to simulate easing without ever changing the Ease value. Create at least a 20-frame Motion Tween of a symbol moving across your Stage. Now add a keyframe in the middle of the tween and move it close to the beginning of the animation. If you test your movie, you'll see that it has a similar effect to setting an Ease value for the tween. The difference is that you have more control over this style of easing. You can move that middle keyframe closer to the beginning or end of the tween to get different effects. You can also add more keyframes and move them around to see what happens. Just make sure that you add keyframes after the tween is in place for the trick to work properly.

   TEXT BLOCKS, THERE'S ROOM FOR EVERYONE

All the same font

Two fonts in same field

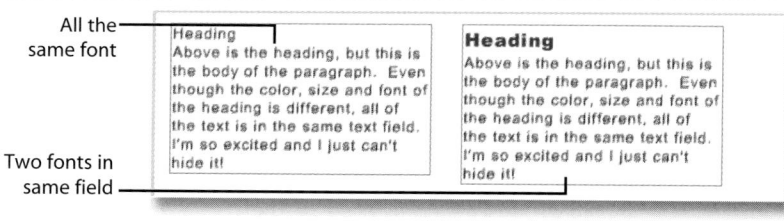

Text fields are often underestimated. Many of their features go unused or unnoticed by the average user. One of these features that can be very useful is the handling of more than one font in a given field. Start by creating two or more lines of text on your Stage within the same block. Highlight one of the lines of text and leave the other unselected. Now, using the Property inspector, change any of its properties. This can be very helpful if you want to highlight code in your text as I do in the book `like this` without having to create several fields and position them individually.

You'll have to make good decisions about when to use this method because it can cause delays if you want to quickly change your fonts.

BITMAPPED TYPE

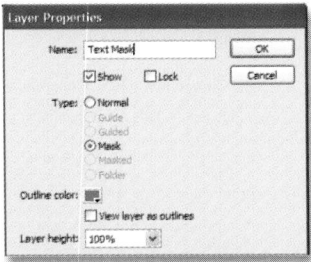

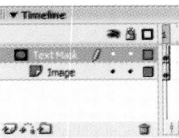

Painting text with a bitmap image could seem like an advanced task at first. Here's how to make the advanced, very simple by using a mask.

Create a layer named "Text Mask" and place the text you want on the Stage. Create another layer named "Image" and place a bitmap or anything you'd like to show through your text on that layer. Make sure the "Image" layer is under "Text Mask," double-click the "Text Mask" layer, and change its type to Mask. Now change the "Image" layer's type to Masked. Finally, make sure your text is right over the image and lock both layers to preview the effect. This is a rather impressive outcome considering the small amount of work required to accomplish it. Oh, and I recommend using very bold text to make more of the image visible.

 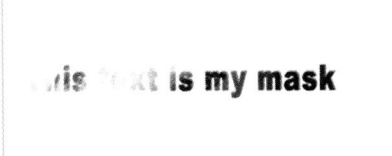

 RESIZING TEXT FIELDS

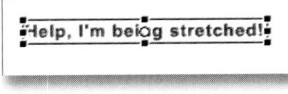

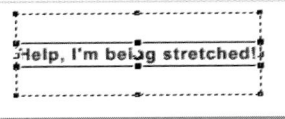

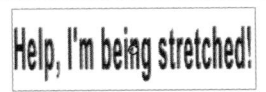

There has been a lot of discussion about text fields in this book. There are several tips on changing the size of text blocks and what not. The only thing we haven't talked about is how to actually scale text (stretch it). To do that, just activate the Free Transform Tool, select the text block, and go to town. Guess what? The text field is still editable after you've stretched it all over.

That was a quick tip, wasn't it? Didn't even take long to read. I like that.

I'M FADING FAST

With the introduction of behaviors in Flash MX 2004, a simple fade is an easy thing to create. Okay, that's great, but these behaviors aren't going to work in every situation. What if you wanted a shape to morph into another while it fades out? Not going to happen with a behavior.

The great thing is that even without behaviors, fading effects aren't difficult to create. Create a simple Motion Tween (must be tweening a symbol). On the last keyframe, go to the Property inspector, click the Effects button, and set the Alpha to 0. That's all there is to it. Now you have a basic fade-out effect.

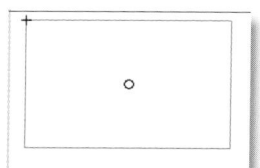

The same thing applies for a Shape Tween. You can use the tip about See Through Shapes to set the right Alpha for a shape. Use behaviors when you can, but keep this one under your hat for those customized situations.

   ## THERE'S TOO MUCH PRESSURE

If you're using a drawing tablet to create artwork in Flash, you're one of the lucky ones. I love these things because they give you a much more natural sense of control over your drawings. Flash even steps up to help you make what you draw as natural as possible.

With a tablet installed, activate the Paintbrush Tool in Flash and look at the Use Pressure option just under the word "Options" on the right. Activating this option will tell Flash to sense the amount of pressure you're using while painting, giving your strokes a more natural look. I know several animators who would never use Flash if it didn't have this simple feature. If you don't see the option I'm referring to, then you'll need to go out and buy a tablet to see it.

SUPER FAST TWEENING

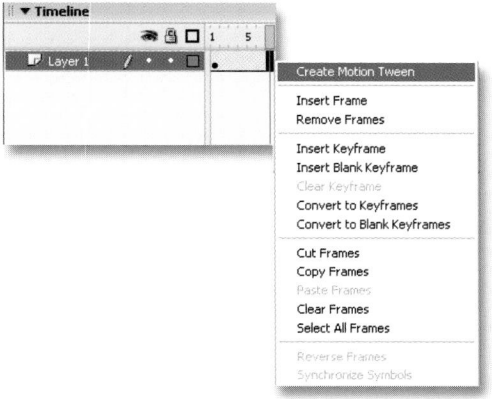

There are several actions that we repeat over and over when creating a Flash movie or application. Creating a tween is arguably at the top of this list. That being true, it would only make sense that there would be a super-fast way to create these crazy tweens. Also, it appears that the people at Macromedia have decided that Motion Tweens are even more common than Shape Tweens because this tip only works for Motion Tweens.

If you right-click (OPT-click on Mac) any frame in your Timeline, at the top of the list of options you'll see "Create Motion Tween." Selecting this option will quickly create a Motion Tween for that span of frames. Super fast!

SEE-THROUGH SHAPES

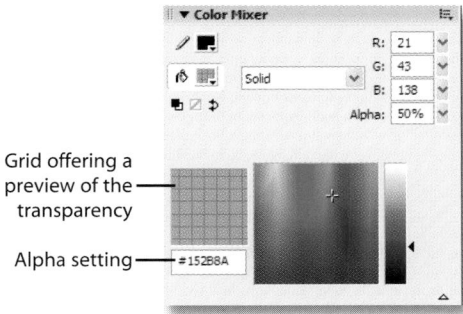

Grid offering a preview of the transparency

Alpha setting

If you've ever wanted transparent text or shapes without going through the hassle of converting them to a symbol first, then you're not alone. Transparency is a fun setting to play with, and it's very easy to do so. When choosing a color (stroke or fill), instead of using the options in the Toolbar or the Property inspector, look at the Color Mixer panel (SHIFT-F9). Turn any color transparent by choosing the color and setting the value in the Alpha field to something below 100%. The lower the value, the more transparent your color will be. You're even given a little grid underlay so you can preview how transparent the color will be. Now just apply the color as you normally would and bam! Instant transparency without converting to a symbol.

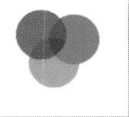

  LET FLASH FOLLOW YOUR LEAD

From time to time, I hear about crazy situations where a person has a tween set up, and they decide to add a keyframe to change it somehow. Okay, it's not crazy—it's a pretty common thing, and everyone has needed to do it occasionally. You could do the typical adding of a keyframe to the tween and then move your item on the new frame, but you can do it even quicker. Here's how....

Set up a tween and select any frame in it. Now simply move the object on the Stage to where you want it. Look at the Timeline and you'll see that Flash has added a keyframe for you. No need to even use the pesky keyboard for this one. Flash behaves as any good servant should—it anticipates what the master wants and does the work for the master. That'll do, Flash. That'll do.

   DEGREES IN EVERY DIRECTION

Using the Line Tool isn't the most difficult thing to do. You basically just drag the line you want between two points and there it is. It can be hard to create certain angles, though.

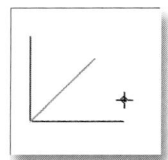 So, try holding down the SHIFT key while creating a line, which will enable you to draw lines on any 45-degree angle. You can draw perfectly flat horizontal lines, vertical lines, or a 45-degree angle directly in between. Just another little tip to help take the guesswork out of making your visions come to life.

MULTIPLICITY

For the most part, when you want to create a tween of any kind, you select a frame in a frame span and set the Tween option in the Property inspector. However you decide to apply your tween, one thing seems to remain true. You can only create one tween at a time. In actuality, you can add many tweens at once by simply selecting multiple frames that are in different frame spans.

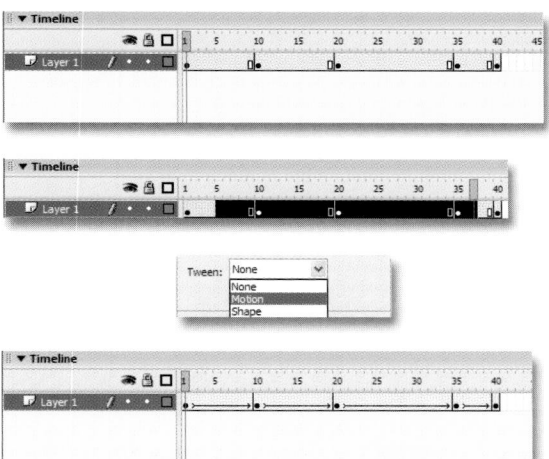

NOTE: A *frame span* is a series of frames between two keyframes.

If you have multiple frame spans that you'd like to animate quickly, just select frames across each span you want to animate and set your Tween in the Property inspector as you normally would. Immediately, all frame spans selected will have the tween applied. This can save a lot of time in a case where you have many layers that have keyframes set properly and just need to be animated. Yeehaw, another time-saver!

   NOW THAT'S SHAPELY

It's a common thing to select some artwork and press F8 to convert it to a symbol, but did you know that you also can convert a symbol instance back into a shape? Select any group or symbol instance on the Stage and press CTRL-B to execute the Break Apart command. This will essentially break the object apart, leaving behind only what was inside of it. So if you had a symbol instance of a circle that was just a shape, then you'd convert that instance back into the shape.

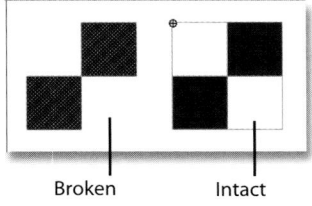

Broken   Intact

This can be tricky, though. For instance, if you have an object with many other objects inside of it, and you break it apart, you'll end up with all those objects on your Stage. To make sure that you break it completely into shapes, you can simply press CTRL-B over and over until you see that only shapes remain.

 ANIMATION TO SYMBOL

Nesting is placing animations inside symbols and symbols in symbols and so on…. It's always a good idea to make use of nesting as often as possible. I for one have often gone off the handle and been so carried away by my wonderful work that I forgot to create a symbol to contain it. I'm sure I'm not alone, right? But it's one thing to convert a selected object that's not moving into a symbol. It's something different to convert an entire timeline. Or is it?

To convert any timeline to a symbol, press CTRL-ALT-A (SHIFT-CMD-A on Mac) while viewing that timeline. You'll notice that this selects the entire timeline and everything on it. Now

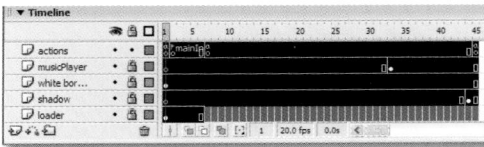

press CTRL-ALT-X or OPT-CMD-X on Mac (Cut Frames), then CTRL-F8 to create a new symbol. Name the symbol and press OK. This takes you to your new symbol's timeline. Once here, select the empty keyframe on Frame 1 and then press CTRL-ALT-V or CMD-F8 on Mac to paste your cut frames into the new timeline.

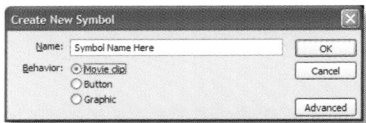

You'll have to clean up your original timeline a bit because it will have empty frames from the cut, but other than that, you're done.

 LETTER BY LETTER, I'LL KERN THEM ALL

More and more of you are coming to Flash from a print production background. You're used to using InDesign or Quark, and for many of you Flash is a strange world. Although Flash certainly lacks the text layout power of any good print production program, it does have a little-known ability that could go overlooked. Typically when you select a text field, you are able to set Auto Kern on or off to let Flash adjust the spacing between each letter itself. However, let's say you need only certain letters to have more space between them than others.

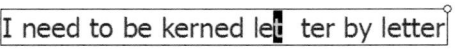

Create some text on your Stage and select an individual letter. Go to your Property inspector and set the Character Spacing value to 20. Doing this will increase the spacing for that character alone on its right side. You can adjust any letter's spacing to get your own customized kerning. The only problem is that there is no way to save the kerning settings for a letter or font, so you'll have to do this for each letter all the time. It is helpful though, isn't it?

    EVEN SHAPES NEED A HINT

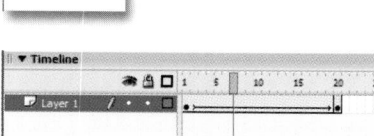

In this book, you've heard the term "hint" several times. Normally it has referred to ActionScript. Until now. There is another type of hint in Flash known as a shape hint. Here's an example showing how it works.

Make sure Snap to Objects is enabled, and then create a square on Frame 1 of your Timeline. Now add an empty keyframe on Frame 24 and place a circle of similar size to the Stage. Add a Shape Tween to the frame span so it will morph from a square to the circle. Watch the animation and see how Flash morphs from one to the next. Now go to the first keyframe of the tween and press CTRL-SHIFT-H (SHIFT-CMD-H on Mac). You'll see a small red circle with an "a" in it appear. This is called a shape hint. Press CTRL-SHIFT-H again. Drag the "b" circle up to the bottom-left corner of the square until it snaps in place. Drag the "a" to the bottom-right corner. Go to Frame 24 and drag the "b" to the top-right edge of the circle and the "a" to the top left. They should snap in place and turn green to indicate that they're set.

When you replay the animation, you'll see that the same animation morphs in a whole new way. Flash matches the point of each shape hint on each keyframe to that of the next. This enables you to actually control the way your shapes animate. Add as many hints as you like and right-click any of them to remove one or all of them. Doesn't get much more powerful than that.

CHAPTER 4 • Create Better Effects and Animations **71**

STAY INSIDE THE LINES

Brush Mode button

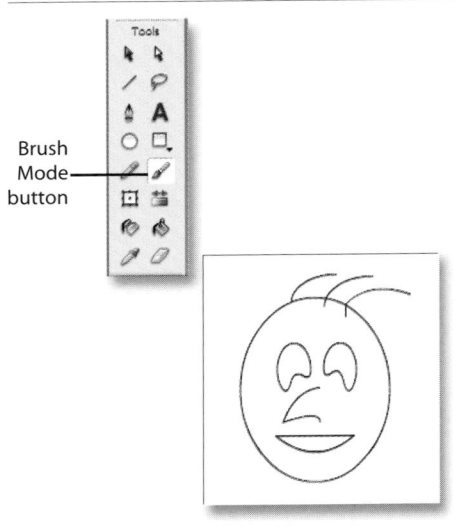

Painting with Paint Inside mode active

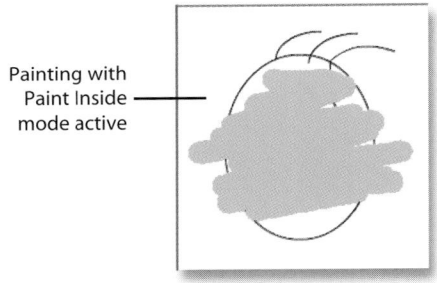

I bet you heard this a lot when you were a child. I actually still have people telling me this as an adult. Scary, I know. Luckily, there is a nifty little option that will make staying in the lines a piece of cake when you're creating artwork in Flash.

Create any outline of a shape without a fill color. Activate the Paintbrush Tool and look at the Brush Mode option at the bottom of the Toolbar. Choose Paint Inside, and as long as you start your brush stroke inside the lines, you can scribble as much as you like without ever going outside the lines. Where was this feature when I was doing *Highlights* magazines?

Make sure your outline (stroke) is connected so that Flash can properly determine what the inside is. Oh, and there are other cool Brush modes too. Play with them as well. Also, try starting your brush stroke outside the outlines of your object, and you'll see that Flash will paint only "outside" the closed shape. It's almost as if Flash is treating the outside as an "inside." Weird, huh?

FLIP IT, FLIP IT GOOD

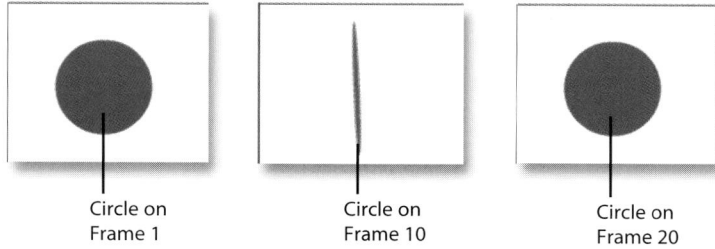

Let's just cut right to the chase on this one. Draw a circle on Frame 1 of your Timeline and convert it to a symbol by selecting it and pressing (F8). Add another keyframe on Frame 20 and add a Motion Tween to the span of frames. On the final keyframe, select the circle instance, go to Modify > Transform, and choose Flip Horizontal. Now watch your animation and you'll see that a nice little coin flip effect is in place.

Of course, you don't have to use this tool for animations only. It can be very helpful when you just need to flip a symbol to face in another direction. And don't forget the Flip Vertical command that appears right next to it.

Circle on
Frame 1

Circle on
Frame 10

Circle on
Frame 20

Feel the Flow

Speedy Tips

Raise your hand if you would like to learn how to create the same animations, the same sites, and the same effects in half or even a tenth of the time. Oh

Feel the Flow
Tips to Help You Work Faster

come on, someone has to raise their hand. Oh, wait, I'm not there, so I can't see you raise your hand. Tell you what, take a picture of you with your hand up and send it to me. Better yet, invite me over for a nice dinner, I'll present the question, and you can raise your hand then. Okay, I'll wait for the invite. While I'm waiting, I'll assume that at least one or two of you raised your hand. This chapter is chock full of those little gems that all the power users want to know about any program they use. Everything within these next few pages will speed up your workflow so much, you will burst into flames and your friends will watch and laugh as you sit there on fire. Mom, you were right—I'm not normal.

  QUICK SWITCH TABBER

Flash MX 2004 introduces a very helpful feature known as *tabbed documents*. We've seen this concept in several other products, and now we're lucky enough to have it in Flash as well. It allows for relatively fast switching between your various Flash documents. But I have a secret. There's actually a faster way to cycle through your documents. Faster, you say?! Isn't that what I just said? Anyhow, if you want to quickly cycle through your open documents, use CTRL-TAB, and with each press you'll jump to the next open document. It doesn't get any easier or faster than that. That is, until they come out with a mind-reading input device. Sorry, but this one is only going to put a smile on your face if you use Windows. The Mac OS X version doesn't support tabbed windows.

  POWER PANELS

For all you power users out there! That's right, for everyone who thinks a mouse should never need to be touched (except for drawing, I hope), this one's for you. Normally, to collapse, expand, or go to a particular panel, you'd have to make an exception and use that horrid mouse. But why not just use CTRL-ALT-TAB to quickly cycle through the panels one at a time? The active panel will have a white dashed outline around its title to let you know it's active. To expand or collapse any active panel, just press the Spacebar. Now that's powerful stuff.

Oh, if you're on a Mac, don't bother with this one. Due to interface differences, it doesn't apply to you.

   THIS LOOKS LIKE A JOB FOR... SUPER ZOOM!

No, I haven't created a new superhero whose weapon of choice is a magnifying glass. Although you may feel like one after reading this brilliant tip! Activate the Stage area of any Flash document by clicking anywhere on. Now hold down CTRL-SHIFT and scroll the wheel on your mouse up and down. When you scroll up, Flash zooms in; when you scroll down, Flash zooms out. The best part about this is that the zoom is centered on wherever you have your mouse located, so you can control the focus of the zoom by moving your mouse around while you scroll. Now you are the new superhero, so go fight crime and dance in the streets.

Sorry, but this one doesn't apply to people without a mouse wheel or people using a Mac.

    HERE'S A SHORTCUT

Duplicate button

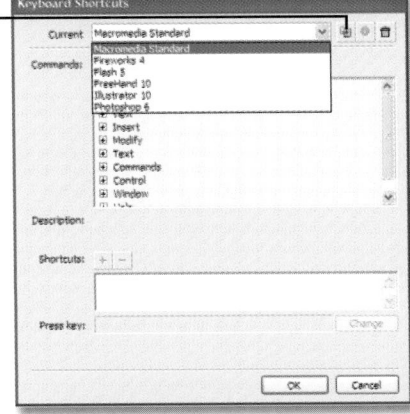

A number of people who are new to Flash usually have experience in some other programs that have certain similarities. After using these programs for some time, they may have adapted to the keyboard shortcuts for that particular program. If you're one of those people, chances may be that Flash has similar shortcuts by default, but if not, then you have some options.

Go to Edit > Keyboard Shortcuts and you'll see that Macromedia has given you a few predefined shortcut sets to choose from. And if that isn't enough, just choose the set that's closest to what you like and use the duplicate button to make a new set of your own. Now you can safely define each command as you will by selecting the command from the tree, selecting the Press Key field, and pressing the key combo you want to set it to on your keyboard.

    ONE STEP FORWARD, ONE STEP BACK

Moving through a Flash Timeline while in authoring mode is most commonly done by using your mouse to jump to a particular point or scrub across frames. Of course, you can also press ENTER at any time while the Timeline is active and it will begin to play through. Both of these methods are great, but if you want to slowly step through the Timeline frame-by-frame, you might be at a loss for how to do so. Feel lost no more, my friend. You may think that using your arrow keys would do the trick, but no, those are for nudging objects on the Stage. To quickly step through the Timeline one frame at a time, use the "," and "." keys on your keyboard. The "," key moves left and the "." key moves right. An easier way to remember these guys is to think of them as "<" and ">" instead of "," and "." because it makes more sense visually. Just remember that you don't have to hold SHIFT for this to work.

   UNSELECT ALL

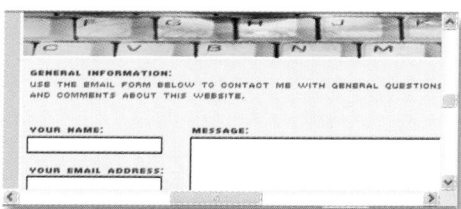

There are about a thousand different ways to select artwork on the Stage in Flash. You can use the Arrow tool and drag, or CTRL-A (CMD-A on Mac) to select everything at once. You can also select individual items in a variety of ways that I could go on and on about. Don't worry, I have no intention of doing that. Now let's say you want to make sure nothing's selected anywhere. I'm sure there's been the occasion where you were trying to use the arrow key in the Actions panel and you ended up moving some object you didn't even know you had selected on the Stage. Well, to prevent this in the future, simply press the ESC key on your keyboard to unselect anything you may have selected. This is effective for objects on the Stage as well as your Timeline. Ah, now you can relax. That is, of course, if you can remember to hit ESC.

   TEMPORARY ARROW TOOL

You're late for a deadline, so you're flying through your document, zooming, scaling, and editing all over the place. Your friends watch in amazement as you move faster than their eyes can see. The thing they don't know is how upset you are that you have to look at the keys briefly while you jump back and forth between the Rectangle Tool and the Arrow Tool. You wanna move even faster? While using any tool, try quickly holding down the CTRL key (CMD on Mac) and Flash will temporarily switch you to the Arrow (Move) Tool. When you're done moving an object, you can switch back to your active tool by simply releasing the CTRL key. With this increased productivity, you meet your deadline, your friends weep in awe of your speed, and you can go home with a smile on your face and recommend this book to every human being you meet. Life is grand!

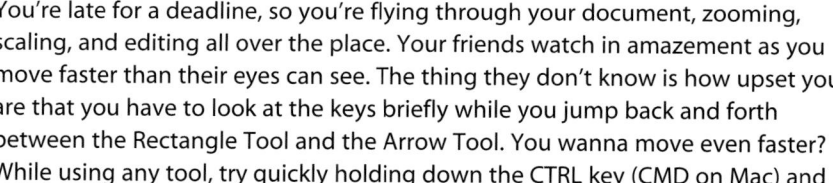

   STICKY HAND

It can be cumbersome and annoying to have to scroll your Stage when you want to see another part of it. Okay sure, you could switch to the Hand Tool (Pan) by pressing H on the keyboard, but if there's an easier way, do it. That's my motto. Like many things in Flash, a quicker way exists. If you are using your mouse to move objects around your Stage and need to instantly pan to see a different part of the Stage, just press and hold the Spacebar, which will temporarily switch you to the Hand Tool. Now click anywhere on your Stage and drag. Your Stage pans each time, which is why I refer to this little guy as the Sticky Hand. It reminds me of the way Tom Cruise grabs those screens and slides them in *Minority Report*. Well, without the mouse, that is. I bet they used Flash to make those screens!

   BY THE POWER OF MYSKULL!

If you want to be a true power user and switch from tool to tool in Flash without bothering with the mouse and Toolbar, then you'll want to make note of some of the most important key shortcuts. Okay, so important may be the wrong word, but certainly the most used. They are V, Arrow (Move/Select); T, Text Tool; Q, Free Transform; and Z, Magnifying Glass (Zoom).

Of course, there are many others as well, but you can discover any tool's key shortcut by rolling over it and waiting for a second. Flash will display the key command for you to add

Move/
Select

Text
Zoom

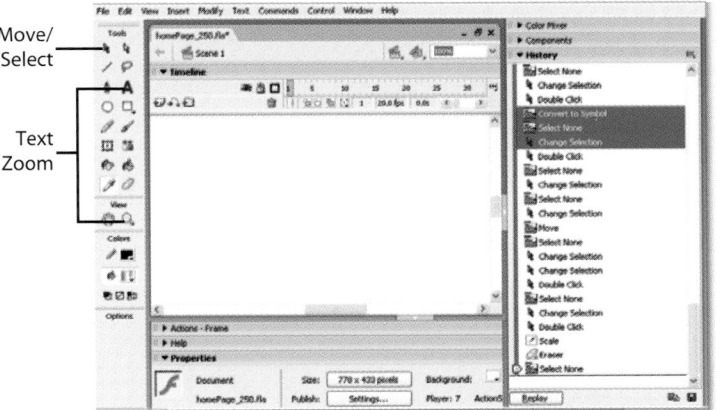

to your list. Who knows, if you get good enough, you may not even need to have the Toolbar there at all. Oh yeah, and if the tool has more than one option like the Rectangle, you can cycle through them by pressing the key over and over.

   AND... KEY TIMELINE

I've mentioned several ways to use your keyboard to make working in Flash easier and faster. The only thing is that most of these shortcuts had to do with the interface or tools. But what about the Timeline? Good question. The most important keys of all to remember in Flash are those that allow you to quickly edit the Timeline. The only difference is that with these you'll need to use your mouse on occasion to ensure you are on the right layer or frame. So without further ado...F5 is Insert Frame(s), SHIFT-F5 is Remove Frame(s), F6 is Insert Keyframe(s), SHIFT-F6 is Clear Keyframe(s), and F7 is Insert Empty Keyframe(s).

Notice that there is no SHIFT-F7. That is because a blank keyframe is still considered to be a keyframe and therefore you'd just use SHIFT-F6 to clear it. Attention! If you memorize nothing else, memorize these. Going to the menu system every time you use one will make your life way more complicated than it needs to be.

   SO MUCH TEXT, SO LITTLE TIME

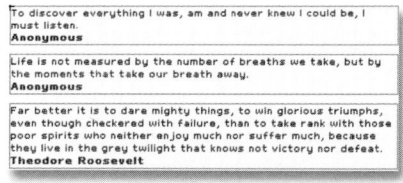

Okay, so you have several text fields on your stage. Some are big, some Arial type, some bold, and you want to quickly change them all to 12-point Courier. Although you could spend the next twenty minutes selecting each field and setting it accordingly, why bother with all that work? All you have to do is select multiple text fields at once and then go to the Property inspector. Here you can change any property of those text fields all at once as if you had only one selected.

Font field

You may see some dashes "––" in some of the property fields. This indicates that the multiple fields you have selected have different settings for that property. Just ignore it and choose what you will.

ZOOM, ZOOM, ZOOM…

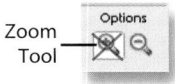

Zoom Tool

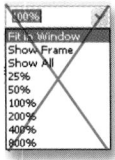

Zooming in and out can be one of those things you do over and over without having a quick way of doing so. Switching to the Zoom Tool takes two steps, as does selecting the zoom factor from the drop-down at the top right of the Timeline. Like many other commonly used actions in Flash, there are a couple of nifty keyboard shortcuts to help you zoom in and out in only one step. Using CTRL-+ and CTRL-- (CMD+ and CMD- on Mac) to zoom in and out will make your life a great deal easier. There is one catch to this, though—unfortunately, you cannot use the + and – keys on the number pad section of your keyboard. Life is full of tradeoffs; I guess this is just one of them.

IT'S TIME TO FONT-CYCLE

Picking the right font is usually a complex system of trial and error. Because the average user has over 50 fonts on his/her computer, we need to make that trial process as simple as possible. Place any text field on your Stage, fill it with some text, and make sure it's selected. Now look to the good old Property inspector and instead of clicking the down arrow for the list of fonts, click in the box with your cursor. This activates the font list box so that all you have to do now is use your up and down arrow keys to cycle through the font list. As you do this, you'll see your selected text box change in real time so that you can quickly pick the font you want and see what it looks like in place at the same time. Freaky how easy that was, huh?

Just think of the time you save by not having to open the font list and choose one each time to preview it. Yikes, I shudder at the thought.

  QUICK EDIT

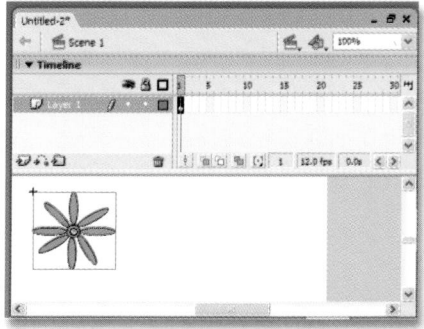

If you need to edit a symbol and you have an instance of it on the stage somewhere, hang on, because it's going to be a complicated process. Here's what you do… Double-click the symbol instance. Yep, that's it. If you double-click any instance on your stage, you will be taken to the Timeline of the original symbol so you can edit it. Of course there are other ways to edit a symbol, but as I said, this one is the fastest for editing in place. I remember long ago when this feature didn't exist. The horror!

   LAYER LOCATOR

It can be very easy to lose track of what layer a particular object is on. This is especially true when you're rushing to get something done and aren't really paying attention. Not that I've

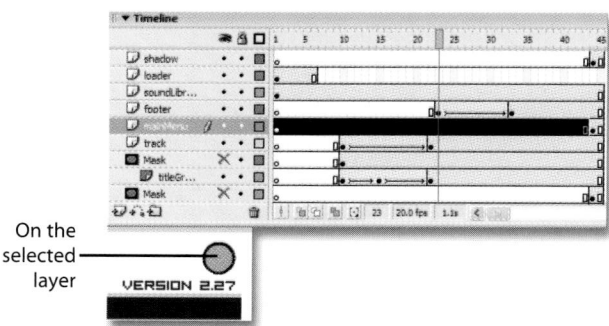

On the selected layer

ever done that, but if it happens to you, there's an easy way to determine what layer something is on. Just select the object or shape in question and look at the Timeline. The layer that is highlighted in black is the layer that contains your object. Okay, so you have the information—now what you do with it is up to you.

     TWO BIRDS, ONE PANEL

Open the Transform panel, if it's not already open, using Window > Design Panels > Transform (CTRL-T or CMD-T on Mac), and then select any object on your stage. In the Transform panel, enter a new scale, rotation, skew, or some combination thereof, and then press the Copy and Apply Transform button at the bottom of the panel (the one on the left). Look at that—you now have a copy of what you had selected with the transforma-

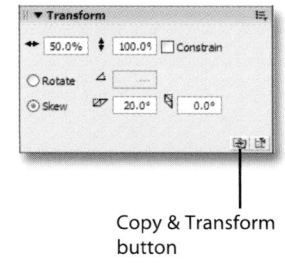

tions you entered applied to it. This will really help save time for those of you who love to enter exact amounts for your trans-formations.

Copy & Transform button

Make sure that you don't press Enter while your cursor is in any of the fields in the panel or your changes will be applied without making a copy (unless that's what you want). Oh, one last thing…Don't deactivate the Transform panel before applying the changes or you'll have to start over.

     THE BIG FIVE

There are five very basic, very common things that everyone must deal with when creating Flash content. I call these "The Big Five." Pretty clever, huh? That's cause I'm supa smawt.

Anyhow, these five basic activities should be easy to perform, and you shouldn't have to spend a lot of time doing so. Here are the big five along with their keyboard shortcuts to save you some time. I suggest you memorize these. Or not.

1. Document Properties (CTRL-J) (CMD-J)
2. Flash MX 2004 Preferences (CTRL-K) (CMD-K)
3. Publish Settings (CTRL-SHIFT-F12) (OPT-SHIFT-F12)
4. Publish (SHIFT-F12) (OPT-SHIFT-F12)
5. Test Movie (CTRL-ENTER) (CMD-ENTER)

Of course there are many other shortcuts that are equally important, but these are the basic biggies.

   NO CLONING LAYERS

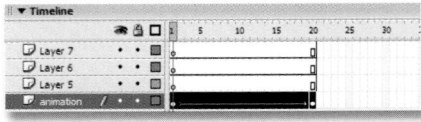

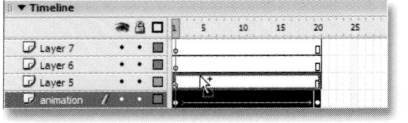

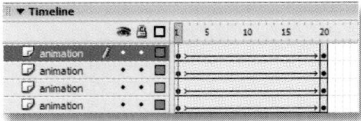

You guessed it. There's just no easy way to duplicate a layer. Oh sure, you can duplicate almost anything else with a couple clicks, but I guess layers just aren't as important. Well, I disagree with that, so I'm going to help you out.

Select the layer you want to duplicate and then click the Create Layer button at the bottom left of the Timeline. Now, select all frames of the layer to duplicate by clicking that layer's icon. Finally, drag the selected frames up to the new layer while holding the ALT key (OPT key on Mac). Release your mouse button and you'll see that you now have an exact copy of your layer.

I must say that even though that wasn't very hard, I really think there needs to be a Duplicate Layer button somewhere. But what do I know?

   QUICKEST COPY IN THE WEST

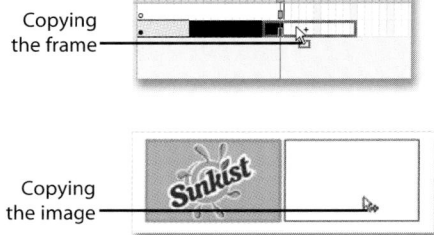

Copying the frame

Copying the image

Copying objects or frames in Flash is not so hard to begin with, but there is an extremely easy and quick way to do it. If you simply hold down the ALT key on the keyboard (Hold OPT on Mac) while dragging any object or any frame(s), Flash will copy whatever you are dragging to the new location instead of moving it there. You can tell a copy is being made when your cursor changes to display a tiny plus sign (+) next to your pointer.

QUICK SPAN SELECT

This frame span selected by double-clicking

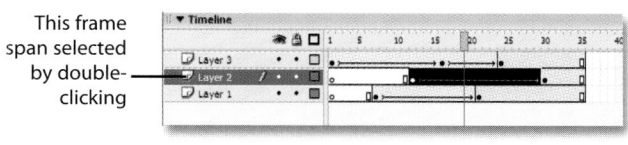

Moving entire segments of your Timeline, such as a set of frames, is a common task. It can also require some rather good hand-eye coordination if your frames are at the default size and you're working on two hours sleep, as I've been known to do. Instead of clicking and dragging to select a particular segment of your Timeline, just double-click a frame in the Timeline and it will select all frames in that frame span. Now you can easily move the block of selected frames around your Timeline. You may remember this style of frame selection (called span selection) from the old Flash 5 Timeline. The only difference is that in Flash 5, you only had to click once.

Be careful while using span selection this way. If you have a tween in place, double-clicking like this will not select the last keyframe for that tween. So you could end up breaking a good tween if you're not paying attention. To include the last keyframe as well, hold down the SHIFT key when double-clicking. See, there's always a solution.

   QUICK CREATE

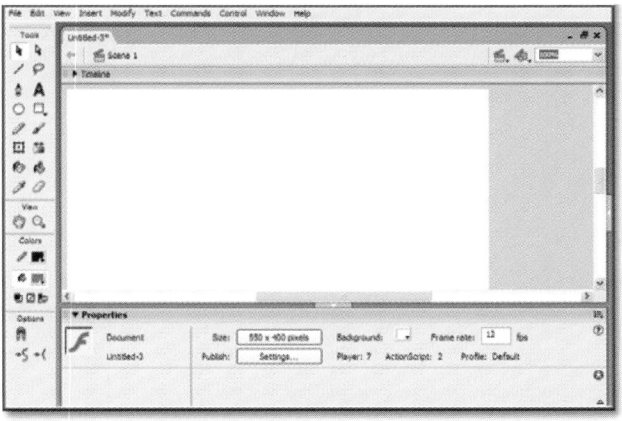

Remember the old days when pressing CTRL-N in Flash meant a new document instantly? In Flash MX 2004, this same shortcut prompts you with a window that lets you select the kind of document you want to start with. Being a long-time Visual Studio developer myself, I do take comfort in the familiarity here, but I hate having to click the OK button in this dialog just to get a new document open quickly. If you want instant gratification too, try this. Instead of CTRL-N, press CTRL-ALT-N (OPT-CMD-N on Mac). This will skip the new New Document window and immediately create what you want. A new blank document.

   ## GET OUT FAST

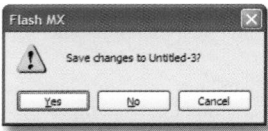

If you look at my workspace at any given time, you'll probably find five to ten files open. When it comes time to close a file, it really annoys me that I have to go to File > Close for each one, so instead I do this…. Press CTRL-W to quickly close the document, and then when you're given the typical pop-up asking you if you'd like to save the document, press the first letter of the choice you want to make (y:yes, n:no, c:cancel).

I know, I know. This one isn't one of those super tricky, ultra-secret tips that you'll faint over, but it can certainly save you a lot of time.

   ## TRACKING

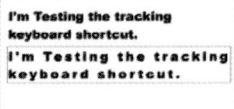

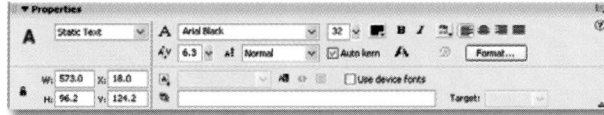

Skydivers might think we're talking about sweeping your arms back and flying. Well, we're not. Tracking in terms of text (as we mean it) refers to the horizontal spacing between characters. If you've ever increased or decreased the tracking for a block of text the old-fashioned way, then you may be used to the "trial and error" concept. Usually you'd select the text and change the tracking value in the Property inspector.

There's an easier way. Select the text block and press CTRL-ALT-RIGHT to increase and CTRL-ALT-LEFT to decrease the tracking of the selected fields. Now you can keep your eye on the field instead of jumping back and forth a million times. Oh, and to quickly reset the tracking to 0, press CTRL-ALT-UP (CMD-OPT-RIGHT/LEFT/UP on Mac). It's not flying, but it certainly speeds things up.

MULTIPLE INSERTIONS

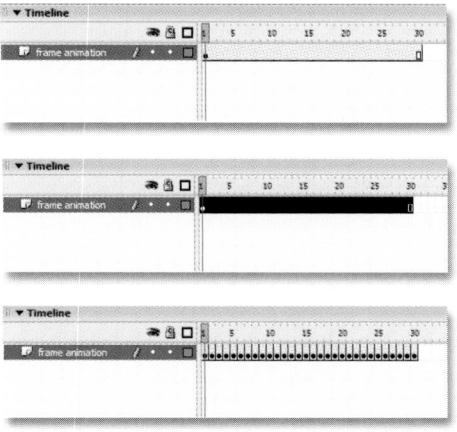

There are several options you have when you are inserting frames in the Timeline. You can insert a keyframe, frame, or blank keyframe. Although this is usually done one frame at a time, there are also those situations when you may want to insert multiple frames at once.

Try selecting a span of frames in the Timeline and pressing F6. You'll see that every frame selected is converted to a keyframe. This can be especially handy when working on intricate frame-by-frame animations the way many traditional animators do. The same thing works for F5 (Insert Frame) and F7 (Insert Blank Keyframe), so be sure to try those as well.

PASTE IN PLACE

Copying and pasting objects to different locations in your document can be frustrating. I'm so used to just using CTRL-C (Copy) and CTRL-V (Paste) in Word or other programs that I always assumed things would be just as easy in Flash. Not that copying and pasting is hard, but there is a little trick to make things more predictable. It may seem that Flash pastes your object in an arbitrary position on the stage, but actually things are pasted dead center of the stage by default. The good thing is that this is not the only way to paste. Another option is to press CTRL-SHIFT-V (or CMD-SHIFT-V on Mac)—Paste In Place—when pasting to paste the object at the exact coordinates you copied it from.

This method only works when using Flash alone, so don't try to grab something from Illustrator and have it pasted in place. How would Flash know what place it started?

    QUICK, UNDO ALL

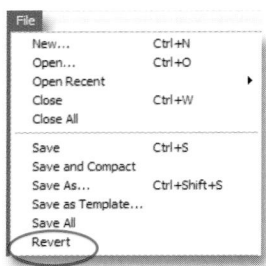

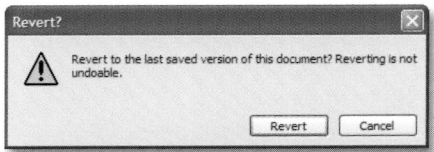

Ever made hundreds of changes to your document, only to realize that you don't want to keep any of them? If this happens, you have several options. You can hold down CTRL-Z and hope you didn't make more changes than you have the ability to undo. You can close the file without saving and re-open it. Or, here's a new one. Go to File > Revert, and your document will revert to the state it was in when you last saved it.

It's kind of like when a writer balls up a page he hates and throws it in the trash. The only difference is that we don't have a page, so we use a menu command. It's not quite as romantic, but it works nonetheless.

    IN AND OUT, ONE BY ONE

Selected by holding SHIFT

It's not always so easy to select multiple objects on your stage at once. The typical tool for this is the Arrow Tool, which lets you create rectangular selections, but that's not always going to cut it. A nifty thing to remember when you want to make multiple selections is holding down the SHIFT key while the Arrow Tool is active and just selecting each item by clicking them one at a time. This will keep all the objects included in the selection. You can also unselect items individually by clicking already selected items while holding down the SHIFT key. So simple, yet so useful.

   TAKE INITIATIVE

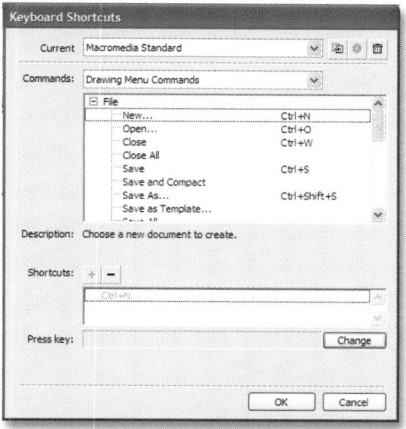

A lot of times, complex animation or editing programs come with a cool reference sheet that lists all the important keyboard shortcuts to help you learn. When you've practiced enough with the program and become familiar with the keys, you can put the reference sheet away and go about your business. I'm a big fan of these sheets, as you can pin them up right by your computer until you are comfortable. Unfortunately Macromedia doesn't provide you with this sheet.

I recommend you make your own if you're just starting out. Go to Edit > Keyboard Shortcuts (Flash MX > Preferences on Mac) and look through the defaults, writing down all the combinations that you use most often. Now you have your own customized sheet without all the keys you never use. Hey, you should be an author!

   IS IT A SYMBOL?

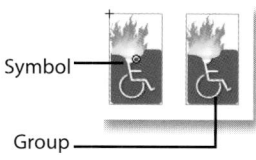

Symbol

Group

When you're working fast in Flash, you want to take the guesswork out of any situation. One of the biggest things designers wonder about is whether an object on the Stage is in fact a symbol, group, shape, or just a text field. Because anything can be nested in a symbol, it may be hard to tell. Sure, you can always look at the Property inspector for the information, but if you keep it hidden, that may not be the easiest way. So here's the deal. If you select something and it is outlined in a light-blue rectangle, then you know it's either a group, symbol, or text field. Shapes are highlighted in gray when selected.

If it's a symbol, you'll see a small circle appear in the middle of the object. Yep, it's that easy. There is one thing to remember, though—you must have the Arrow Tool active to when selecting the object in question. This may not seem like a ground-breaking tip, but I chose to include this because many people aren't aware of this fact, and it can save you a lot of time and eye movement. And who wants to have to move their eyes? I mean, jeez!

Island of Misfit Tips

Cool Tips

There are literally hundreds of killer tips throughout this book. Hence the name, "Killer Tips." And while most of them have a wonderful home called

Island of Misfit Tips

Miscellaneous Tips

"A Chapter," there are some tips that are misfits. These tips are on an island where they can all sulk in their loneliness, just like the toys in that Rudolph claymation movie. Come on, let's sing the song… "Why am I such a misfit? I am not just a nitwit. You can't fire me; I quit, since I don't fit in. Why am I such a misfit? I am not just a nitwit. Just because my nose glows, why don't I fit in?" Brings back memories, doesn't it? Anyhow, even though these tips are misfits, they have found a home here, and they are no less important or spectacular than any of the other tips, so love them just the same. Basically, I'm asking you to give these tips a new home in your heart.

   FAILED TO SAVE ERROR!

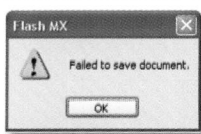

Yikes, I've been working for hours on this file, and when I go to save my beautiful changes, I get an error saying that Flash Failed to Save the document. What now? Sorry, nothing you can do. Just start over from scratch. I'm kidding. First off, don't panic, and whatever you do, don't close Flash or the document. This issue is usually encountered when you're working on a file that has been opened from a network share that was momentarily disconnected. Regardless of why it happened, here's how to save your work.

First try to use the File > Save As option and save the file to your local hard drive. If you still get an error when saving locally, create a new document and begin dragging all your Library items from the old file to the new. Then go to your main Timeline, click anywhere on your Stage, and use CTRL-ALT-A to select all frames and artwork. Copy and paste frames (using CTRL-ALT-C, CTRL-ALT-V respectively) into the main Timeline of the new file. Disaster avoided!

   DASHES TO DASHES

A broken Motion Tween

A broken Shape Tween

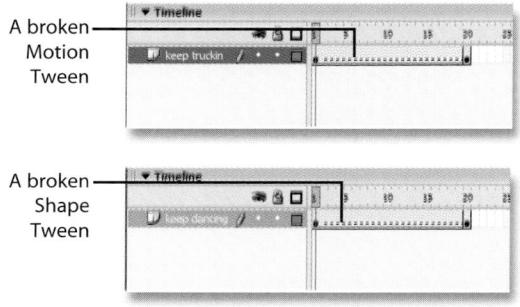

Say you create a wonderful tween on your Timeline, but something's off. It isn't working the way it should, and you see dashes across the tweened frames. Now what? Going to the Property inspector reveals an exclamation mark that, when clicked, says, "Motion tweening will not occur on layers with ungrouped shapes or on layers with one or more group or symbol" or "Shape tweening will not occur on layers containing symbols or grouped objects." The solutions are as simple as the error messages. A proper Motion Tween can only have a single symbol on the keyframes involved in the tween. A Shape Tween can only work when there are raw shapes on all keyframes involved with it. This means no groups, text fields, symbols, or anything that's not raw artwork

I'm sure that if you double-check your tween, you'll find that you've violated one of these rules. My advice… "Don't." Locate the frame(s) that are causing the problem and remove the unwanted items. When you get it right, your dashed line should turn to a solid arrow line.

  ## WARNING WILL ROBINSON

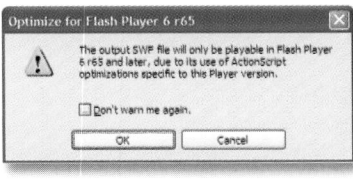

There are many occasions where you'll perform some action and be prompted with a warning telling you of the dangers involved. The great thing is that a lot of these warnings come with a check box enabling you to specify whether you ever want to be warned about this kind of thing again.

Sometimes I get a little cocky and uncheck the "warn again" box without reading the warning at all. I just want to be left alone. Later I find that if I'd paid attention, I wouldn't be up until 5 AM fixing something. If you have done this and want to turn a warning back on, go to the Warnings tab under Preferences (CTRL-U) and pick the ones you are missing. This is also a good place to turn them all off at once. Just be careful because some of them are very helpful. Or so I've heard.

   ## START FROM HERE

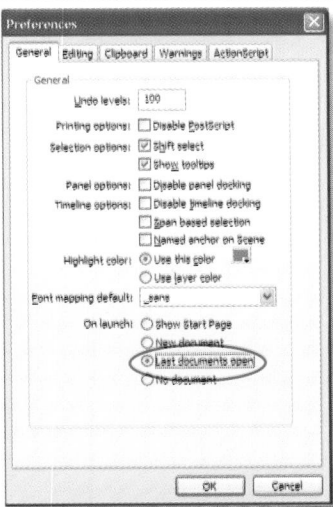

Wouldn't it be nice if you could open Flash and have it automatically load all the files you had open the last time you closed it? I think so too.

Open the Preferences window (CTRL-U), and at the very bottom of the General tab you'll find some options enabling you to choose what happens when Flash is launched. The default option is Start Page, but the one that comes in handy the most for me is "Last Documents Open." Now you know, and knowing is half the battle, GI Joe!

   TAKE IT TO THE LIMIT

A lot of people feel as though they really take Flash to the limit of what it can handle. Which prompts the question, "What are the limits of Flash?" Good question, I'm glad you asked. There are two fixed limitations when it comes to what a single Flash document can handle. First of all, you cannot have more than 16,000 frames in any one Flash document. This number refers to the total number of frames in the entire movie, not just one timeline. The other restriction is that you cannot have more than 16,000 symbol instances in any one document.

Although it's very rare that a developer would need to exceed these limits, it does happen from time to time. If that's the case, you'll need to link multiple movies together with an ActionScript command such as `loadMovie`. Oh, and feel free to let me know if you need to exceed these limits. I'd love to know the reason why.

   BUTTON CLICKS AND ALL THAT JAZZ

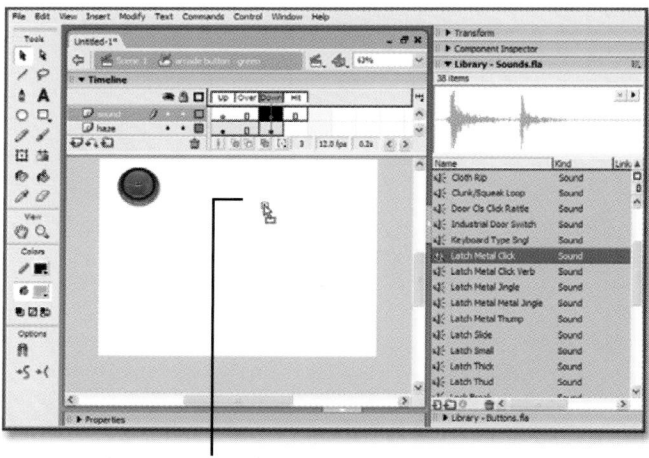

Mouse cursor is dragging the Latch Metal Click sound from the Library to the Stage

Buttons are especially fun things to create. They serve many purposes, and you can do a lot with them to add flare. One way to add flare to a button is to have it respond with sound as the user interacts with it.

Go to the Timeline of any button symbol and create a new layer called "Sound." Create a keyframe on the sound layer at the "Down" frame. With that keyframe selected, drag a sound from your Library onto the Stage.

Test your movie, and you'll see that anytime you click the button, your sound will play. You could also move the sound from the Down frame to the Over frame to have sound play when you roll over the button.

There's not much to it, and the right sound effects on a site can make all the difference.

SECOND TO LAST RESORT

Flash isn't perfect, and from time to time you can run into a problem that doesn't seem fix-able. Maybe the panels keep disappearing, or you get weird error messages from time to time. Before you decide to give up and reinstall Flash out of frustration, try one more thing. Delete your user preferences. You can find the folder at the location that corresponds to your operating system and delete it.

Windows 2000/XP:
C:\Documents and Settings\<username>\Local Settings\Application Data\Macromedia\Flash MX 2004\en\Configuration

Windows 98/ME:
C:\WINDOWS\Application Data\Macromedia\Flash MX 2004\en\Configuration

Mac OS X:
<Macintosh HD>:<*username*>:Library:Application Support:Macromedia: Flash MX 2004:en:Configuration

…where *username* is the user's short login name.

The next time you start Flash, it will rebuild your preferences and may fix whatever problem you were having. If that doesn't work, then you guessed it… Reinstall time!

   ## PREVIEW A MOVIE CLIP WITHOUT TESTING

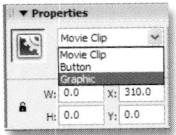 Let's say you have a movie clip nested within your Flash document in a place that takes a few clicks to get to when you're testing your movie as an SWF file. Now let's say you are making frequent changes to that movie clip and need to keep seeing the results of those changes. It's a major pain to continually test your movie and then click through or wait to get to where that clip plays. Here's a nifty trickaroo to help you with a situation like that.

Select the movie clip instance that you need to preview. Look to the Property inspector, and in the drop-down where it says Movie Clip, select Graphic. Now to the right, change Single Frame to Play Once. This changes the behavior of the instance to that of a graphic, and therefore you can preview the animation if the instance is given enough frames on the Timeline to animate. Now all you have to do is preview the movie clip's animation by scroll-ing through the Timeline as if the tween was actually in front of you instead of nested in the movie clip. This trick will not work if the original movie clip has actions or other nested movies in it; it only works in simple situations, but it can still be very helpful. When you're done, change the behavior back to Movie Clip.

   CSS IN FLASH?

Okay, so it's not exactly CSS in Flash, but it's close. Go to your Library and use the panel menu to add a "New Font..." Choose Arial as the font type "Heading 1" in the Name field and press OK. Now add some text to your Stage, select that field, and set the font for it to "Heading 1," which is now listed in your font list with the "*" character next to it. Finally, go

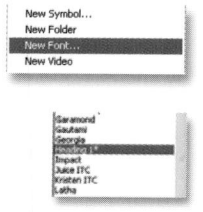 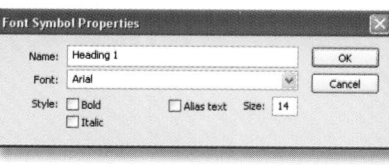

back to your Library and double-click the font symbol you just created. Change its font to something else and click OK. You'll notice that any text fields with type "Heading 1" have changed to the new font.

Essentially, we've created a sort of style that we can change globally at any time. Now, if we have Heading 1 text anywhere in our Flash document, we can change that text with one simple step, instead of hunting down each one and changing them individually. It's sorta like a style in HTML.

  INVISIBLE BUTTONS

Standard button

Invisible button

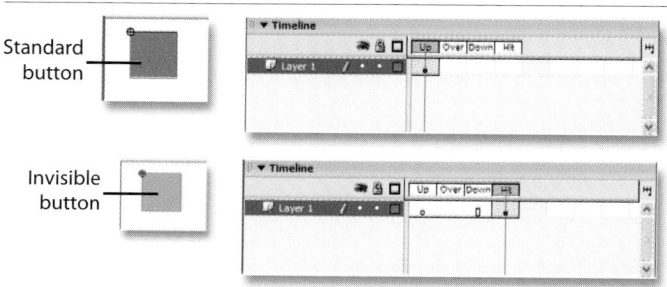

If you've mastered the simple button and would like to move on to something more advanced, check this out. Draw a square on your Stage and convert it to a button symbol (F8). Now, double-click the instance to edit the sym-

bol. Move the first and only keyframe from the Up to the Hit frame. Go back to the Timeline where the button instance was and notice that your button is light blue now. You've created what's known as an "invisible button." Basically, the button itself is invisible when published, but it can still be interacted with. When you roll over it, you see your cursor change, and you can add actions to it just like a normal button. It's useful to place these buttons over another symbol to give them the appearance of being buttons themselves, but without actually having to convert them. Think of it as a hotspot that you can reuse anywhere.

SOUND TRIMMING

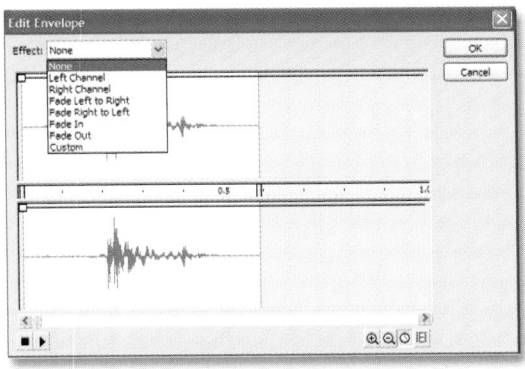

Perhaps a friend gave you a great song for you to use in your movie, but you only need the first part, or you want it to fade in and out. Unless you work with sound and music on computers all the time, you may not have the sound-editing software necessary to alter your sound. Here's what you do….

Select the keyframe where you placed the sound and look to the Property inspector. Click the Edit button to bring up Flash's basic sound editor. Here you can trim the sound by dragging the little gray bars on either end of the middle section. Use the stop and play buttons to test your trimming and the Zoom In/Out buttons at the bottom right to change how much of the sound you can see at once. There are even several built-in effects you can apply to your sound. It's no SoundEdit Pro or Rebirth, but it can do enough to get you by.

   ## BYE, BYE BOUNDING BOX

Maybe I'm on my own here, but when I'm moving an object (Group, Text, or Symbol) around the Stage, the little blue bounding box around it gets on my nerves. It bothers me the most when I'm trying to nudge something around to see what it will look like in position. I have to unselect it each time I want an unobstructed preview and then select it again to move it.

Try this instead: When you select any object, press CTRL-H (Hide Edges) or SHIFT-CMD-E on Mac to make the bounding box invisible. The object is still selected, so you can move it around, but the blue rectangle is hidden. Unfortunately this trick only works for the selected object and is temporary. If you select something else, the bounding box returns, but hey, just keep turning it off when you need to. I think this option should be a setting that sticks, but it's still useful the way it is.

   THE OLD SWITCH-A-ROO

By definition, a symbol instance is really just a dummy item that points back to its original symbol. So when you drag several instances of a symbol onto the stage and then change the original symbol, all the instances reflect the same change. That being said, it only makes sense that you can change which symbol an instance points to, right?

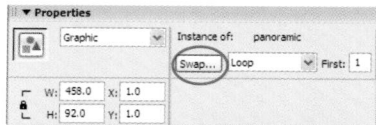

Select an instance of any symbol that's on your Stage. In the Property inspector, press the Swap button. You are given a list of all the symbols in your Library to choose from. Select any other symbol and then press

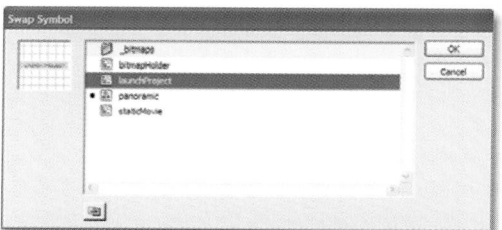

OK to make the swap. Flash has now swapped the symbols that appear on your Stage. In essence, your instance (pointer) now points back to a different original symbol.

The cool thing is that whatever properties you had applied to that instance are still applied. Dat's what I'm talkin' about!

   INSPIRATION

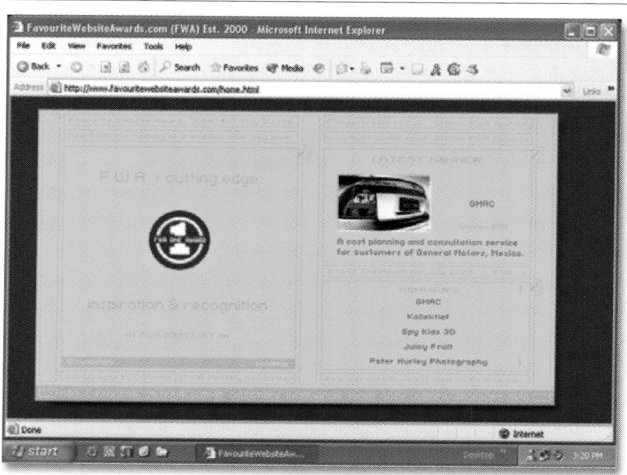

If you want to see what Flash can really do, there's a great place to go. Favourite Website Awards has been around for quite a while, and somehow they manage to always find some of the most compelling Flash sites and animations around. Don't let the content intimidate you. Let it inspire you.

http://www.favouritewebsiteawards.com

 FLASH ACTIVATION

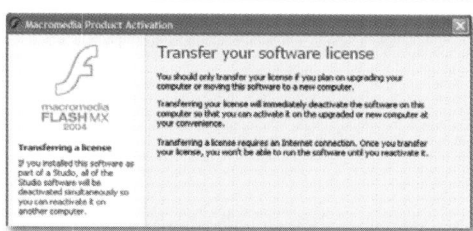

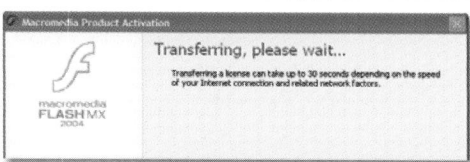

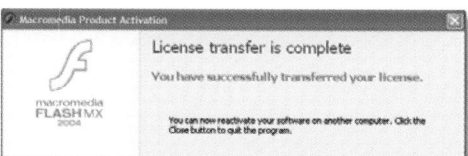

That's right, Macromedia has implemented product activation, just like Microsoft did with Office and Windows XP. Yippee…Not! The standard license for Flash MX 2004 allows you to install the program on two computers. If you try to install it on more than two computers, you'll have problems.

If you want to move an installation of Flash MX 2004 from one computer to another (if you bought a new one or whatever), then you must transfer your software. Go to Help > Transfer Your Software License. This will deactivate that installation of Flash so that you can install it and activate it on the new computer.

I don't think this new method will do very much against piracy, but I'm sure it will serve to annoy all of you to some degree. Enjoy product activation!

 ACTIONSCRIPT.ORG

If you're looking into doing some heavy ActionScripting, you'll definitely want to bookmark this one. You'll find tutorials, forums, mailing lists, and example source material, all at your fingertips. If you need to solve a particular problem, chances are someone has done it before you and is willing to offer you some help. This is a great place to go for that help. Keep in mind, the focus here is on scripting.

http://www.actionscript.org

  THE BIBLE

The very best all-around reference book for Flash is *Macromedia Flash MX Bible* by Robert Reinhardt (© John Wiley and Sons). The focus of the book is nothing like this one, of course. Instead of showing you all the cool shortcuts and tricks, the Bible actually runs you through an in-depth explanation of each and every feature in the entire application. You can either sit down and read through all the tutorials or just keep it on your desk as a reference. Just make sure that you have *Macromedia Flash MX 2004 Killer Tips* by its side. They make a well-rounded pair.

```
http://www.flashsupport.com
```

   HERE'S YOUR KIT

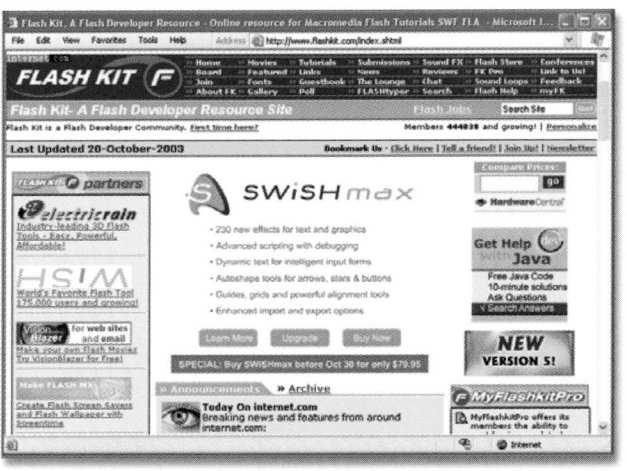

There are literally hundreds of web sites devoted to Flash, and most of them have tutorials and all that, but none is more robust than this one. Flashkit has thousands of tutorials, articles, and lessons, both written professionally and contributed by users. They even have a lot of stuff from the old Flash 4 days if you're still into it. The site is slow at times, but be patient and I think you'll find this is a valuable resource indeed.

```
http://www.flashkit.com
```

  GO RIGHT TO THE SOURCE

Obviously no one can beat the expertise of Macromedia when it comes to troubleshooting Flash. That being said, I thought I'd give you a direct link to the Flash support center at Macromedia. com. You'll find all updated documentation, downloads, components, and technical notes about known problems.

`http://www.macromedia. com/support/flash/`

Oh, and you can go here for user-to-user discussions about any problems you may run into.

`http://webforums.macromedia.com/flash/`

   WE'RE HERE...

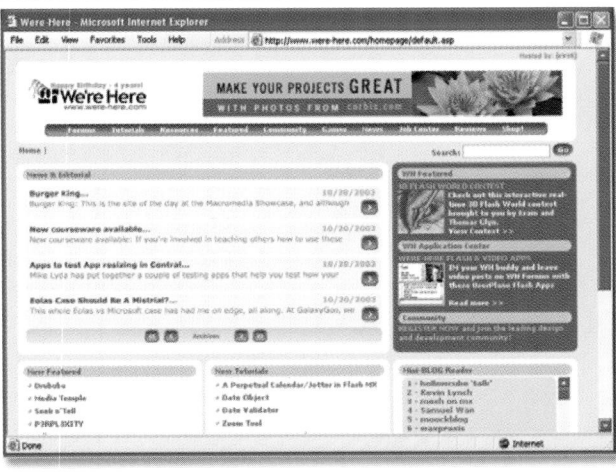

At first it sounds like another sequel to *Poltergeist*, but it's actually a very cool web community for designers like you to mingle and learn. Here's how they describe themselves… "`were-here.com` is a leading online professional resource community for designers and developers, with emphasis on Macromedia Flash technologies." Couldn't have said it better myself. I am "here" quite a bit, so maybe you'll run into me. Or maybe this is reason enough not to stop by.

`http://www.were-here.com`

   ERROR RECOVERY

If you follow the advice offered by this book, you'll never have to worry about losing your work. However, if something major goes wrong, leaving you with only a SWF file of your work, then this may help you. In general, it is impossible to convert a SWF to a FLA file in the case where the FLA is lost and you need to recover your work. There is a solution that can extract source data and code from a SWF file that you can then use to re-create your FLA and save most of

your work. The solution is referred to as *reverse engineering*. Several programs out there will open a SWF and display the data found in it so that you can see and understand all the code and therefore recover any lost work. The best one is Sothink SWF Decompiler (`http://www.sothink.com`).

I have to be honest—I was reluctant to include this tip. It seems that more and more people are using programs like this to steal other people's work. Please don't be one of them.

   THROW AWAY THE KEY

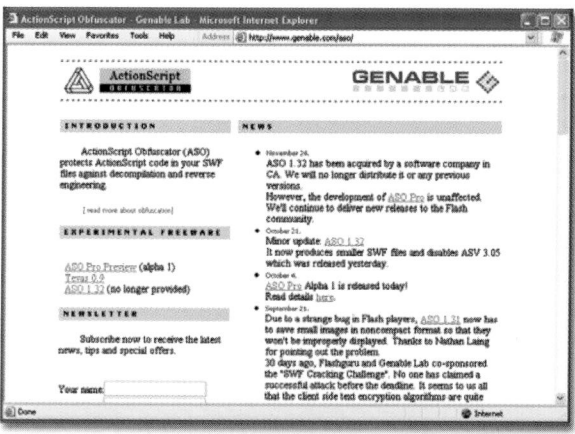

There's a flipside to the Error Recovery tip above. You can process your SWFs so that they are very well-protected. A product called Genable ActionScript Obfuscator was created for the sole purpose of protecting SWF files against decompilation and reverse engineering. If you are sure you'll never need to reverse engineer your SWF files, then go to their web site and get this product so that you can protect your work now and forever.

`http://www.genable.com/aso/`

FLASH ANIMATION

I think by now you've realized that Flash isn't just used as an animation tool. However, if you just learned Flash so you could do your own in-house cartoons and movies, you may want to take a look at this book. Sandro Corsaro has done an excellent job of describing how quality character animation can be accomplished in Flash. This would be the antithesis to ActionScript, but you can't have one without the other nowadays.

The Flash Animator
by Sandro Corsaro
© 2002 New Riders Publishing

Import/ Export Business

Importing and Exporting

When I mention importing, exporting, and templates, I think it's obvious that I'm referring to illegal smuggling of drugs and a phony money press. This chapter is full of

Import/Export Business

Tips on Importing, Exporting, and Templates

tips on how to find the best drug runners and get the top-of-the-line equipment for printing your own fake money. True, it doesn't quite fit in with the rest of the book, but nowadays you have to add an extra bit of incentive if you want to sell a book. Oh, I also threw in a couple dozen tips about Flash templates and the import and export of media and Flash content, but you can skip right past that to the juicy illegal stuff. The only thing I ask is that you give me 10% of all your receipts, and if you're caught, you don't know me and you've never read this book. Deal? Okay, then read on.

   EDIT VIDEO! WHAT'S THAT YOU SAY?

Flash MX 2004 focuses a great deal of attention on making certain capabilities more user friendly and robust. One of the main improvements for you people who import video into Flash is the Video Import wizard. This wizard gives you several powerful options, including the ability to edit the video you're importing. Import a video by using CTRL-R and locating a video file. When you click OK, the wizard starts by asking if you want to edit the video file or just import it. Choose Edit and click Next. In editing, you can create clips based on the original video by dragging the triangle handles on either side of the video Timeline and clicking Create clip. Flash imports several clips based on the original without ever actually altering it.

These new clips are imported into your Flash document, and you can do what you like with them. Granted the editing isn't very powerful, but for the basic trimming of video, this is a handy new tool.

   PUBLISH ME UP, SCOTTY

I like to organize everything. I keep my desktop neat, my Library categorized, and my sock drawer in chronological order by date last worn. Okay, that's not true; my desktop is a mess. Any-

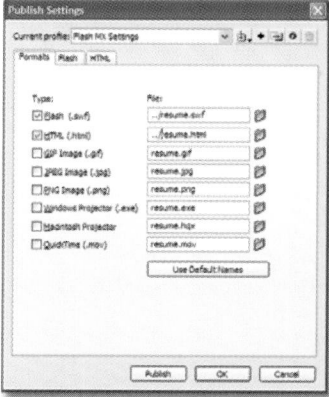

way, if you're like me, then you may want to keep your Flash documents (.flas) in a different directory than your published (.swfs). I for one like to put the FLA files in a sub-directory called "_source" and my SWFs up one level. However, when I publish, the SWFs go to the same directory. So here's a way to have the best of both worlds. Open your Publish settings (CTRL-SHIFT-F12 or OPT-SHIFT-F12 on Mac) and activate the Formats tab, and you'll see a list of filenames that you can publish to. You can choose the folder location by clicking any folder icon to the right, but it doesn't always jump right to the folder above where your FLA is. Put a "../" in front of the filename, and then with every publishing, your SWF will be placed up one level from your FLA. This also works with ..\ and ..: on PC and Macs.

IMPORTING ME STUFF

Have you ever noticed that when simply importing items such as videos and bitmaps, Flash decides to put them on your active Timeline without even asking? But for some reason

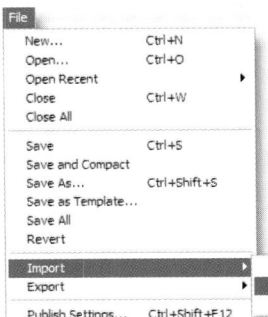

when you import sounds, they jump straight to the Library. Before I discovered this little gem (not that it was hard to find), I would go through the trouble of importing and then deleting the instance of the new asset from my Timeline. Try choosing Import from the File menu and then Import to Library. This will ensure that whatever file you import will be sent directly to the Library and not to your Stage at all. And to make this option more accessible, refer to the tip earlier that discusses how to setup a custom shortcut for Import to Library. You could even use CTRL-R (currently set for Import) because Import to Library is likely better suited and used more often. But hey, that's up to you.

   OPEN AS LIBRARY WAS HERE A MINUTE AGO

Opening a Flash document's Library without actually opening the document itself is a useful option. For the most part, the purpose of doing this is to extract its assets for use in your

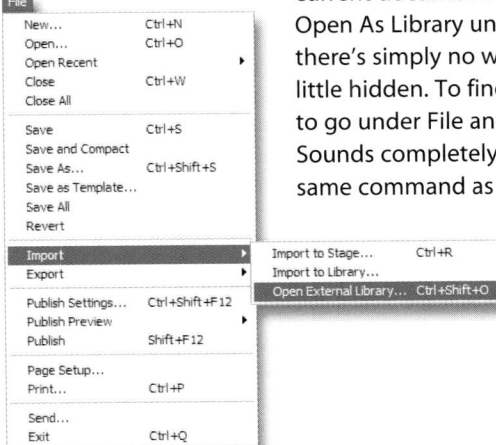

current document. In Flash MX, you would do this by selecting Open As Library under the File menu, but in Flash MX 2004 there's simply no way to do this. Okay, yes there is, it's just a little hidden. To find the same feature in MX 2004, you'll need to go under File and choose Import, then Open External Library. Sounds completely different, doesn't it? Regardless, this is the same command as Open As Library, and if you remembered the keyboard shortcut (CTRL-SHIFT-O or CMD-SHIFT-O on the Mac) from the old days, then you wouldn't even have to bother with this new terminology. Now you know, and knowing is half the battle.

   I CAN'T IMPORT A QUICKTIME MOVIE!

Have you ever tried to import a QuickTime movie and received the following error?

"One or more files were not imported because there were problems reading them."

If so, then you're not alone. In my years of experience and teaching, this is one of the most common errors I've seen since Flash was allowed to import video files. Not to worry though, the solution is simple…Install QuickTime! That's right, if you are getting this error, then chances are you don't have QuickTime installed. For Flash to import QuickTime content of any kind, the application must be installed on your computer. Once you install it, you should not receive this error any more, but instead you'll get the desired video. Keep in mind that this error can occur while importing other files as well, in which case you should check with Macromedia support for specific information regarding your situation.

   KEEP 'EM FRESH

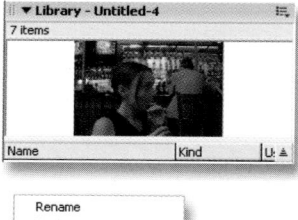

The capability to import bitmaps, video, and sounds into your Flash document is a wonderful thing. However, imported media can complicate things when you're experimenting with your Flash movies. You may have a few bitmaps in place throughout your movie and want to turn them all to black and white images. Unfortunately there's no way to do this using Flash, and it would be a pain to have to re-import and reposition those bitmaps after changing them outside of Flash.

So here's what you do. Locate the bitmap asset in your Library and right-click it. Choose Update from the list of options. You'll see a final dialog enabling you to verify the

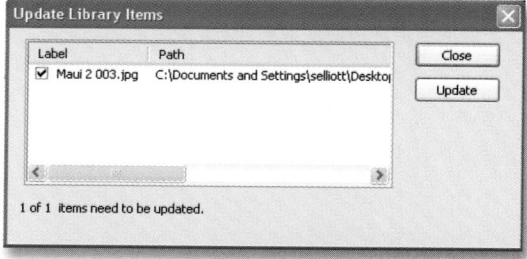

update. Choosing OK here will tell Flash to update your asset with the latest version of the source file. This will only work if the original file is still in the same location. You will get "file not found" errors if you move the .fla file arouund, even if the asset file is in the same relative directory. Hey, nobody's perfect. Except me, of course.

 ## MY FILE IS ALL GROWED UP

Perhaps you've noticed that after working on a single file for a number of hours and constantly saving your changes using CTRL-S (Save), your FLA file is growing in size. This
growth continues even if you just cleared tons of items out of the Library. The reason for
this is that, in Flash, each time you save a file over itself, any changes are appended to the
file, but the file isn't technically overwritten. This means the file size will continue to grow.
In the past, you would have to use Save As and save a copy of the file as a new file to get
the file size down again. Can you say annoying? Flash MX 2004 solves the problem by let-
ting you choose "Save and Compact" under the File menu. This compacts the FLA file and
saves over itself at the same time, giving you a smaller file size while storing any changes
you may have made. I'm still not sure why this isn't the default behavior, but oh well.

 ## ILLUSTRATE MYSELF

Most people who design for the web work with many different vector applications. One of
the most popular ones is Adobe Illustrator, so it only makes sense that I would give you a
tip on how best to import your Illustrator art into Flash.

There are several ways to accomplish this, but the best way is to export your art directly
from Illustrator as a SWF file (Illustrator 9 or later) and then import that SWF file into Flash.
This method provides the most consistent and accurate translation of artwork between the
two programs.

If you're using Illustrator 8, you can still export directly to an SWF, but you'll need to
download the Flash Writer plug-in for Illustrator, which is available at
`www.macromedia.com/software/flash/download/flashwriter/`.

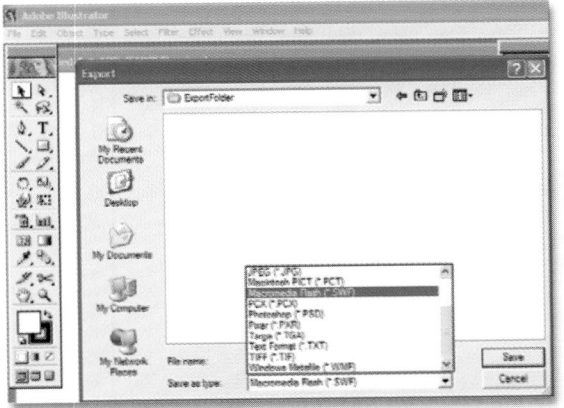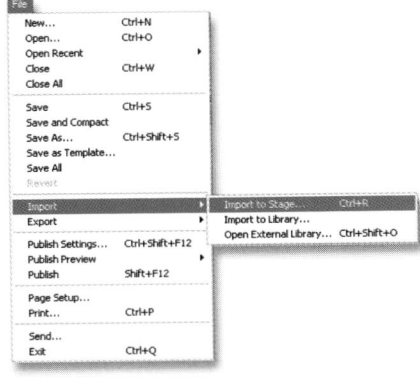

   WORLD SERIES OF IMAGES

When I first started using Flash, the only way to include rasterized video in your document was to import a series of images. When placed consecutively on the Timeline and played back, the images simulate a movie. The problem with that method was always huge file sizes and the constant pain of re-importing those bitmaps. With the new capability to actually embed a video clip directly in your Flash document, there isn't much need for this old-fashioned method. However, occasions can still arise when importing a series of images is preferred or even necessary.

Regardless of your reasons for doing it, the actual process is very straightforward. Simply select the first empty keyframe on the Timeline where you want your sequence to appear and press CTRL-R. Now select the first image in the series and press OK.

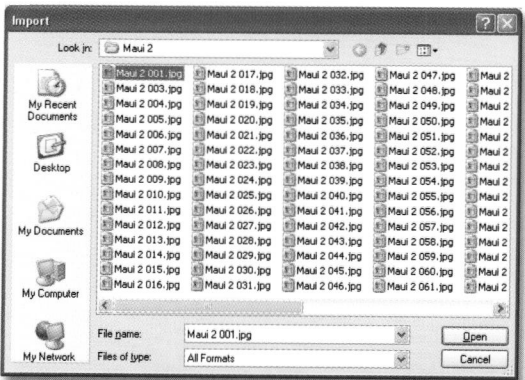

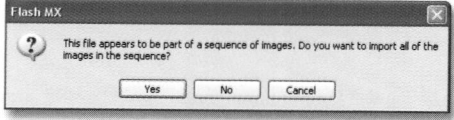

NOTE: The filenames for your series must end with a number and be in numerical order.

When the import process begins, Flash will detect that a sequence of images exists and ask if you would like to import the entire sequence or just one image. Choose Import Sequence and Flash will import all the images, putting each image on its own frame in the Timeline. All the work is done for you, and you have your sequence laid out perfectly on your Timeline. When you test your movie, you'll see that the sequence animates as if it were one long movie.

FILE SWAPPING

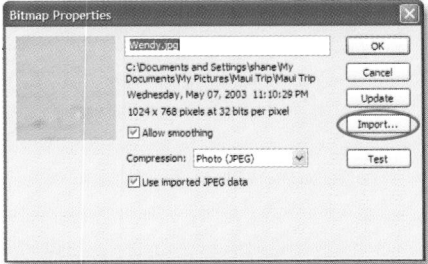

Some of you just became very excited when you saw the title of this one. Sorry, but Flash doesn't support MP3 and file sharing by default. When I say *file swapping*, I'm referring to the Library. If you have any imported assets (video, sound, bitmap) and you placed them on your Stage, you can easily replace them with another file with almost no work.

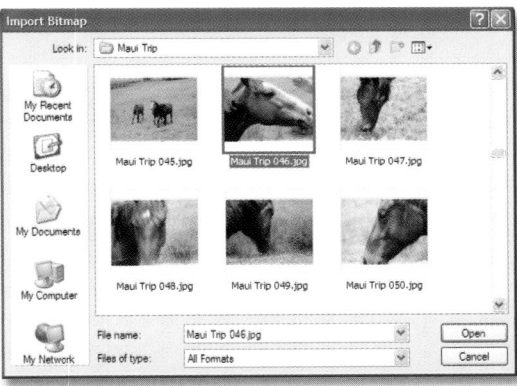

Double-click the asset in the Library and click Import. This will run you through the same process of importing as when you first brought the asset in, but instead of creating a new one, it will just replace the asset with the new file you choose. It's a very useful tool when you have several instances of the same photo and suddenly decide to update the photo with a new picture altogether. The great thing is that you don't have to find each use of the bitmap because Flash does it for you.

 PREVIEW YOUR WORK

Even though Flash has several features built in that let you preview your work while authoring, there's really no substitute for the real thing. Fortunately, there's an easy way to test what you've done without leaving the authoring environment.

Using CTRL-ENTER or CMD-ENTER (Test Movie) at any time while authoring will quickly export your movie to an SWF file and load it in Flash for playback. You can test what you've done and close the window when you're through, and you're thrown right back to your document. This won't always work when you're getting data from a database in Flash, but for everyday purposes it's just what you need.

   NEW FROM TEMPLATE, I MISS YOU!

Okay, first off, it's a little weird that you miss a meaningless File option in a computer program, but whatever. If you used a lot of templates in Flash MX, you likely noticed that the File
> New From Template option is no longer there. In Flash MX 2004, this was replaced with a
much more robust new file dialogue. Go to File, then New (CTRL-N or CMD-N on the Mac) to
open the New Document window. Here you'll find your standard Flash document under the

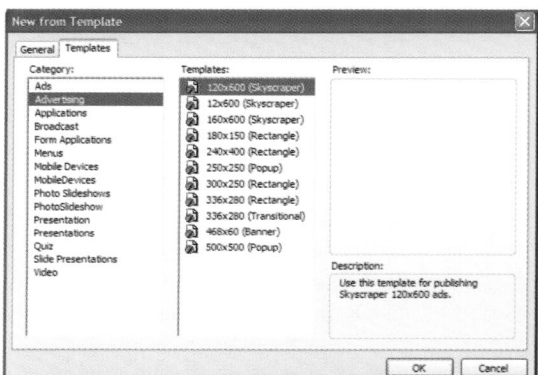

General tab (what most of you will
use), and then a new Templates tab
that lists all your precious templates
from Flash MX, plus some new and
improved ones.

Choosing one of the templates listed
and clicking OK will create a new file
based on that template, just as you
would expect from the old New
From Template command in Flash
MX. I know you'll miss it, but just
think—it's in a better place now.

   MOVIE PROJECTOR

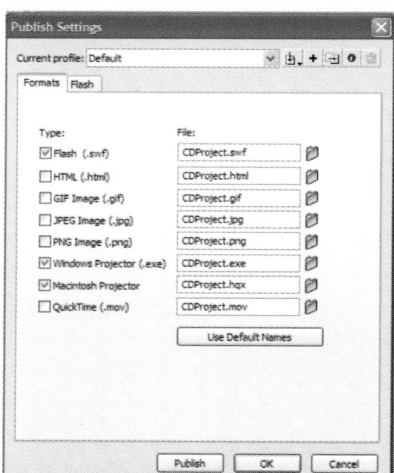

Go to the Publish settings (CTRL-SHIFT-F12 or
OPT-SHIFT-F12 on the Mac) of any Flash document, go to the General tab, and put a check box
by Windows or Macintosh projector, depending on
what type of computer you're using. Now press
Publish (SHIFT-F12). Double-click on the projector
file that was created (either .exe or .hqx file) and
you'll see your movie play without being in a
browser.

Projectors are essentially your Flash movie bundled
with a copy of the Flash player so they do not
require the person running them to have Flash or
the plug-in for playback. They are very useful when
you're sending your movie to someone like my
grandmother who thinks Flash is a part of a camera
or when putting your movie on a CD for distribution.

I'M STUCK WITH FLASH MX 2004—NOW WHAT?

I don't mean to make this sound like a bad thing, but for some of you, it could be. Let's imagine that Flash MX 2004 has just hit the shelves and you were first in line to pick it up.

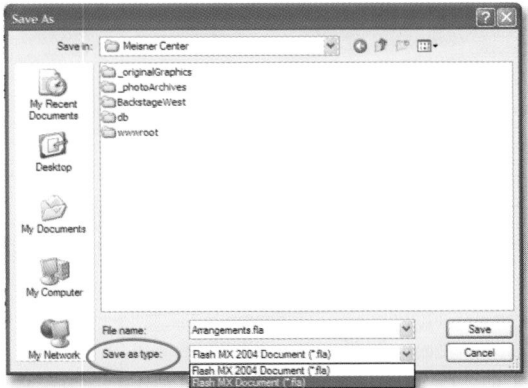

The next day, a client asks you to create a Flash movie and give them the FLA files when you're done, but they only have Flash MX. What do you do?

Not to worry. When you go to save your Flash documents (File > Save or File > Save As), choose to save the FLA as a Flash MX document instead of a 2004 document. You have the best of both worlds, and you can still develop your own cutting-edge stuff in the new format. Now let's say the client wants you to save as a Flash 5 document. You tell them, "Sorry, I'm too cool for Flash 5." You lose the job, but you'll have a great story for your friends. The actual reason is that you are only able to save a FLA file in Flash MX or Flash MX 2004 format.

   ### MAKE MY TEMPLATE

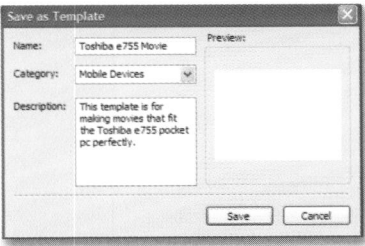

Templates are wonderful time-savers. They give us a place to start because a lot of work is done for us already. You most likely know how to create a new document from a template, but did you know you could create your own templates? Flash templates are just movies that are saved in a particular folder. There's nothing special about them. If you want to turn one of your documents into a template for future use, open that document and go to File, then Save As Template. Give your template a name. Choose or enter a new category, write a brief description, and click Save. The next time you open the New Document dialog, take a look at the Template tab to see your template included right along with all the others.

If you want some pointers on how to best format content in a template file, open some of the existing ones and see what Macromedia has done.

   PASTING NOT ALLOWED?

Copying image data from your clipboard into a document is not really the best way to go about it. This being said, I also know that sometimes it's just necessary for whatever reason.

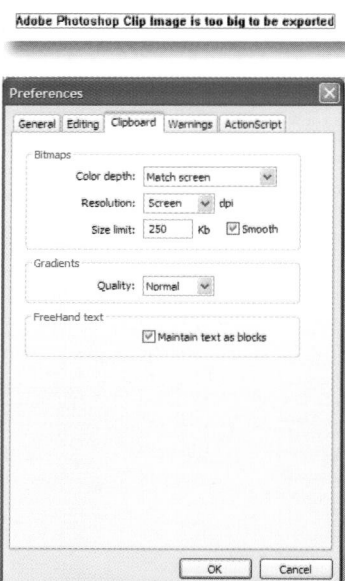

Problems can arise, though, and if you like to copy large images from other programs using copy/paste, then you've no doubt run into this issue. You get an error saying that Flash just can't handle what you got. This is a default limitation to save memory, I suppose. Regardless, in the Clipboard tab under Preferences, you'll see an entire bitmap section just for this issue.

The default size limit is 250K (very small in my opinion), but you can set the value up to 5000KB (5MB) to allow much larger copy/paste operations. You'll see some other options here that don't really need that much explanation. If you have bitmaps larger than 5MB, you'll have to import the image by using File > Import. It's a good idea to play around with the setting to find what works best for your computer. The amount of memory you have installed can have a big impact on how much data can be stored in the Clipboard.

   MAINTAIN ALPHA

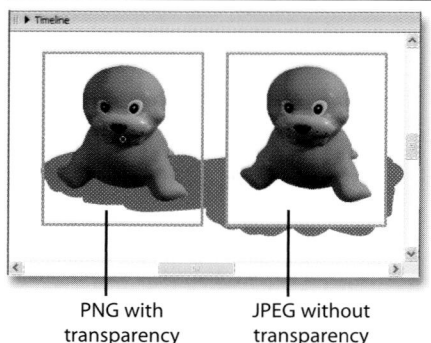

PNG with transparency   JPEG without transparency

Often you have images created in Photoshop or Fireworks that have alpha channels (transparency) and you'd like to keep that when you bring them into Flash. Not a problem. Just make sure that you bring them in using File > Import and that they are a type that Flash imports. Some of the most common are PNG-24, GIF, PICT, and TIFF. Using any of these formats will enable you to keep that transparent background while incorporating it with your Flash artwork.

   EXPORTING "MOVIE MOVIES"

We have the incredible power to import all kinds of video content directly into our documents and work with them as we see fit. The other possibility that is not often explored is the capability to export Flash content as video. There's actually a growing trend where animators are using Flash to create animations and then exporting them as QuickTime movies to put on CDs or DVDs. Not a bad idea.

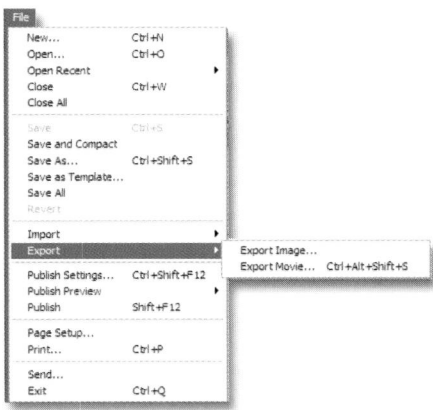

If you're going to do this, remember that there are some basic rules you must follow. First, all of your animation must be on your main Timeline. That means no nested clips, buttons, or other advanced stuff. A great way to see if your movie is going to convert well is to select the first frame of your main Timeline and press ENTER. The Timeline will play back in author mode. If you see everything animate that should, then you're in good shape to export to a video format (QuickTime, AVI, and so on…). If not, then you have a lot of work to do. I hope you read this one before you started because it goes against all typical rules of Flash design.

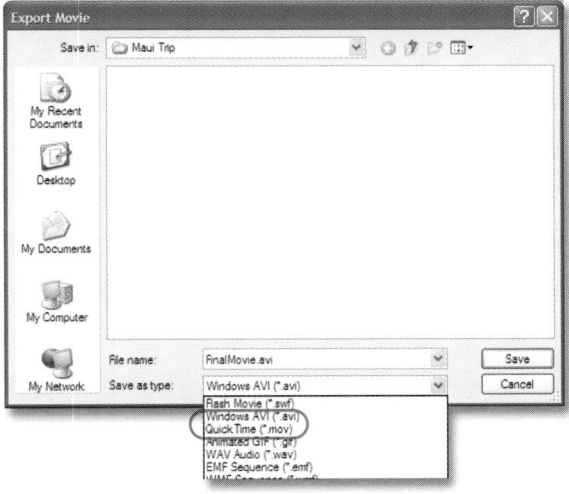

   DIRECTLY FROM PHOTOSHOP FOR WINDOWS

This tip only applies to Windows users, so you Mac people can skip right over this one. Let's say you've been working in Photoshop for years. About 95% of your artwork, graphics, and images are saved in PSD format. You go out and purchase Flash MX 2004 and expect to import some of your Photoshop stuff right into your Flash documents. Sorry, not gonna happen. At least not without some help. To import PSD files directly, Flash requires QuickTime. Because Flash MX 2004 works on OS X, and because OS X has QuickTime built in, there's nothing for Mac people to worry about. If you're using Windows, though, you're going to have to

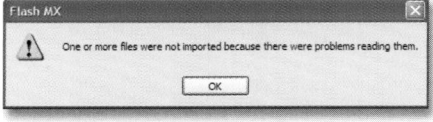

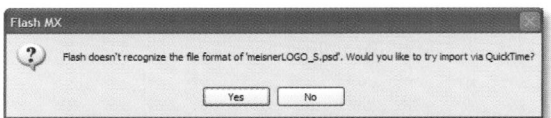

grab the latest QuickTime (demo version is free) and install it. When that's done, try to import that PSD file again and you'll be prompted to let QuickTime handle the process. Answer with a polite "Yes" and you're on your way. No need to run any batch conversion utility.

   MOVIE CLIPS AS THEIR OWN SWFS

Normally, if you were creating separate SWFs for any reason, you would have one source document (FLA file) for each final SWF. You don't have to do things this way though. If you have a movie clip in your Library that would make a really great SWF on its own, you can easily export that particular movie clip as its own SWF.

Right-click (or CTRL-click on the Mac) any movie clip in your Library and choose Export Flash

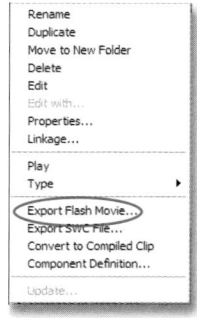

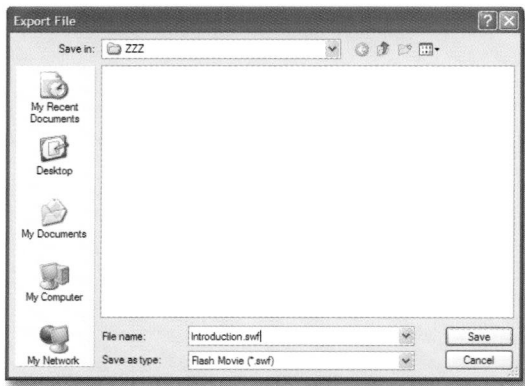

Movie to publish it as its own self-contained SWF movie. To make my life easier, I'll often put several movie clips in one file and export them as files as needed. It's easier to keep track of things this way.

PRIM AND PROPER

There are two ways to get artwork into Flash. One is to copy and paste from another application via the Clipboard. The other is to go to File > Import > Import to Stage (CTRL-R or CMD-R) or Import to Library and locate the file you want to bring in. Which way sounds the best to you? Sure, copying and pasting is much faster, but you can often get unpredictable results.

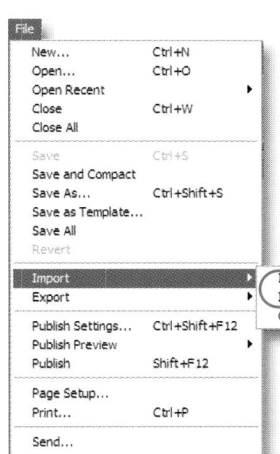

The best way to get any data into a Flash document is by using the Import command. The artwork is run through a more accurate filtering process, ensures very good results most of the time. I wanted to think of a clever rhyme to help you remember this, but I got nothin', so just read it a few times before moving on.

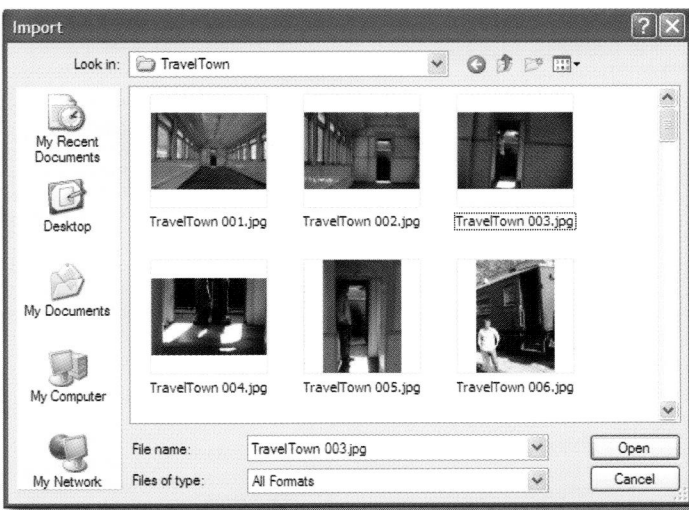

    OVERRIDE YOUR SOUND

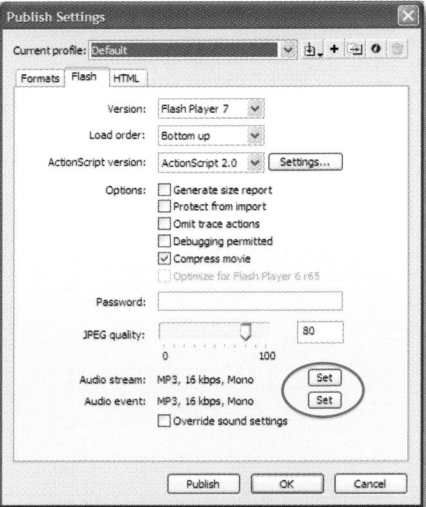

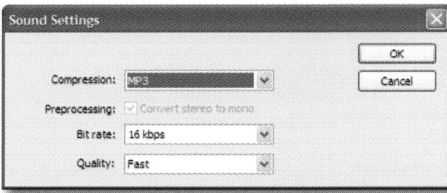

If you've imported sounds or music into your document, each one will be compressed individually. Double-clicking on any sound in your Library will give you the option to change its individual compression settings. This is certainly a much-needed feature, but what if you have hundreds of sounds that you'd like to set to a certain compression? Are you going to double-click each one and change them individually? You can, but you don't have to.

In Publish Settings (CTRL-SHIFT-F12 or OPT-SHIFT-F12) under the Flash tab, you'll find an option at the bottom called "Override Sound Settings," and it does just that. If any sound in the Library is set to Default compression, it will get its compression settings from here on export. You can then set global Stream and Event sound qualities and save yourself a lot of time.

If you are using MP3 audio clips, they are automatically set to use existing compression, so they will ignore these global settings unless you tell them otherwise. You can still compress certain sounds individually for the best results.

   EDIT BITMAPS

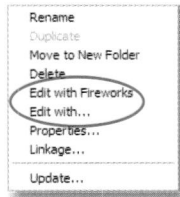

After you have a bitmap image imported into your document, you may realize that it needs some touching up. As you know, Flash cannot edit raster images itself. The cool thing is that it can call on another program such as Photoshop or Fireworks to do the editing for it.

Locate any bitmap in your Library or on the Stage, right-click it, and choose Edit with…. You'll be asked to locate the program with which you want to do the editing, and the specified program will automatically be opened with the bitmap ready for changes. When you're done, save the changes and return to Flash. You'll find that the changes you made are automatically updated in your document.

If you have Fireworks installed, then you can save even more time by clicking Edit with Fireworks instead of Edit with, and Fireworks will be opened, making the process much easier. Hmmm, Fireworks deals with Flash much better than other applications. I wonder if it's because Macromedia makes both applications. Nah, that can't be it.

   LOCK IT UP

I'm all for sharing my ideas, my work, and even my customized code from time to time. This is especially true when it comes to Flash. However, there are some things that are very specialized that I would like to keep private. If you feel the same way, make sure you do this.

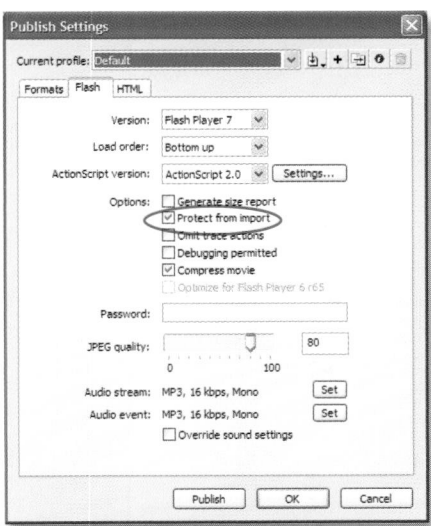

In your Publish Settings (CTRL-SHIFT-F12 or OPT-SHIFT-F12), go to the Flash tab and make sure you check Protect From Import before publishing your movie. This will prevent other developers from loading your SWF into their project and claiming it as their own. It's not a perfect solution because there are a lot of people out there who buy SWF decompiler programs to steal your work, but there's no reason to make it easy for them. It's like a car. If a thief wants it, they'll get it, but you can make it harder for them. I recommend always having this option checked. After all, you can always share your FLAs with the public if you really want to.

   PUBLISH PROFILES

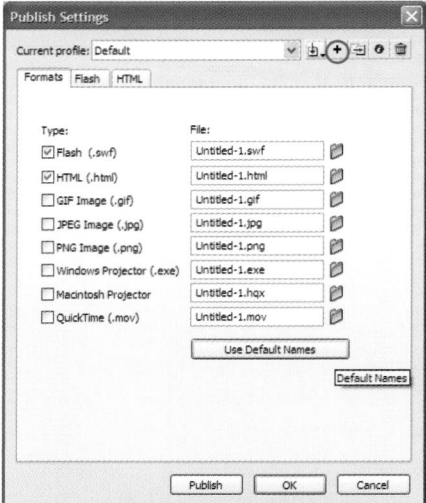

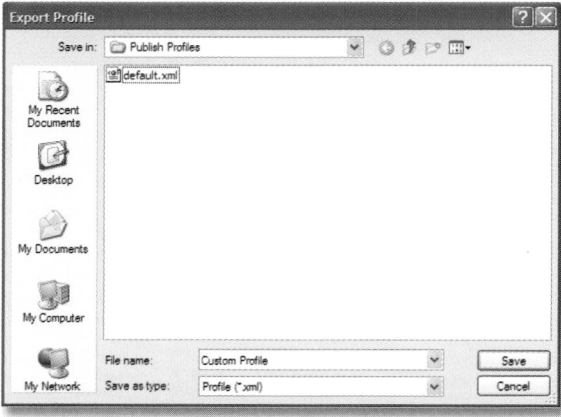

With all the options we're given when we publish our movies, it can be really annoying when you have to change the default settings every time you make a new file. For example, I never use the HTML publish feature. I publish my Flash movie alone and let Dreamweaver do the HTML work. However, HTML is always checked by default, which means I have to uncheck it every time I create a new file. Not anymore!

Go to Publish Settings (CTRL-SHIFT-F12 or OPT-SHIFT-F12) and click the Create New Profile button that has a plus sign on it, name your profile, and click OK. Now choose some formats from the Formats tab, set various options, click the Import/Export button, and choose Export. Now save your profile (it's an XML file) by simply pressing Save. Now you can use that profile over and over to save you the stress and time of remembering all the settings you want and actually setting them.

The only drawback is that your custom profiles are not listed when you start using a new file. You'll have to use the Import/Export button to import one you've saved before. Weird, I know.

GOING HOLLYWOOD

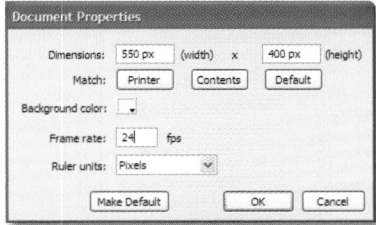

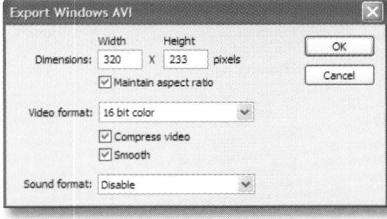

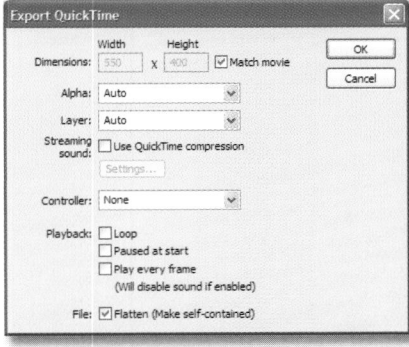

Over the years, Flash has been used for numerous kinds of projects. Lately, developers have added a very exciting type to this list. Flash has been used to create full-length feature animations for video and film. Who knew?

The great thing is that it's not that hard to do. Basically you just create your movie and then export it as a QuickTime or AVI movie, which you can then edit or integrate into any video-editing suite, such as Premiere or Final Cut Pro. The only catch is that you must follow some rules for this to work properly.

First off, make sure all your animations are on your main Timeline and viewable by simply playing through it in author-mode (without using Test Movie or exporting the SWF). Also, do not use movie clip symbols or nest your animations. And do not use actions of any kind. No buttons either. Lastly, set your FPS to 24 or 30, depending on your project.

I also recommend using the Broadcast template that is included with Flash MX 2004. It includes several guides to ensure that your content is within safe margins.

Other settings such as movie size can be determined by looking at what kind of output format you'll end up with (DV, HiDef, and so on…). There are too many possibilities to cover here. Just follow the preceding main rules and you'll be fine.

   BEWARE OF OPTIMIZATION

I know this sounds a little backward, but in some cases, optimizations can cause problems you may not anticipate. For instance, go to Publish Settings (CTRL-SHIFT-F12 or OPT-SHIFT-F12) and look under the Flash tab where it says "Optimize for Flash Player 6r65." This option is only available when publishing to version 6 of the player, but that might be often for a lot of you until Flash Player 7 is widely adopted.

Checking this box will optimize your SWF for version 6 of the player, making it both smaller and faster, but beware. If a person views your SWF after you've enabled this optimization, they will be required to have version 6r65 or higher of the Flash player. If they have an earlier release, they will be unable to see it properly. To be frank, I don't see the point of this optimization because it's so limited. To be Shane, I don't either. I'd say it's best to leave this unchecked, unless you're willing to be release-specific in your site requirements.

Do not
check

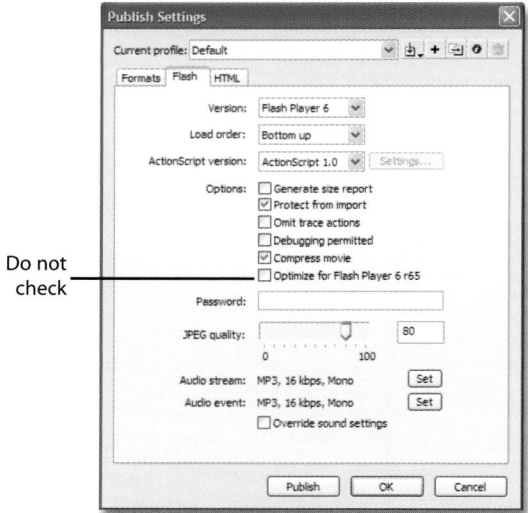

SAVE AS ANNOYING?

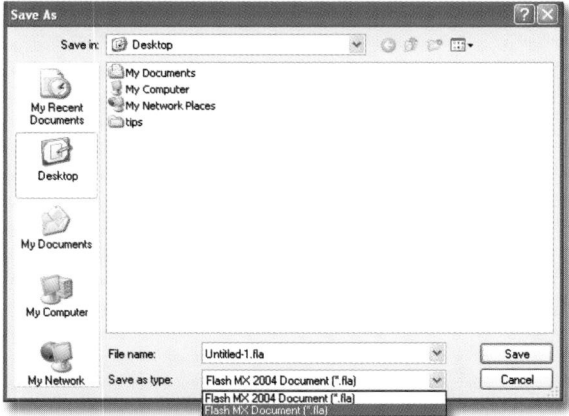

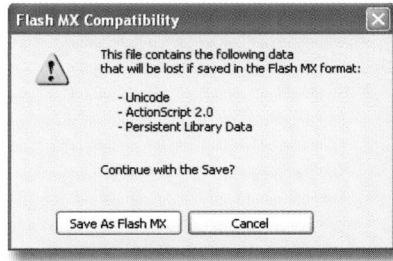

Eventually we'll all be using Flash MX 2004, and Flash MX will be history. In the meantime, you may need to save your work in Flash MX format to stay compatible with those who are behind the times. The good news is that you can do this easily by choosing Save As and then choosing Flash MX as your format. The bad news is that every time you want to save changes you've made to your file, Flash will try to save in the new 2004 format. Do you think Macromedia is trying to tell us something?

Okay, so there's really no solution to this, but here's something that can reduce the annoyance. Save the file as Flash MX 2004 while you work. When you're done and need to share the file with someone still working in the dark ages of last month, you can choose Save As and convert to Flash MX format. Make sure you don't use newer features found in 2004 or you'll lose your work when you convert. Yes, you'll get a warning about Library Data and Unicode, but you can ignore it as long as you haven't actually applied any Flash MX 2004-only features. The warning will show up by default whether you actually have used new features or not.

Use What You Got

You Got

Built-in Component Tips

While I was growing, up my mother always told me two things. Number one, "Don't ever take candy from strangers unless there's money involved."

A

Use What You Got

ps for Built-In Components and Existing Elements

Number two, "Use what the good lord gave you, and if that doesn't work, find someone who has more and take it from them." This is key to understanding the things that Macromedia has provided for you in the Flash authoring tool. There are tricks to using panels more effectively, and secret (seemingly hidden or rarely used) commands throughout the program. My intention in the following pages is to help you to use what is provided for you by making sure you're aware of it and how best to use it. Beyond that, I'll also do my momma proud by teaching you how to take what you're not given so that you'll never go without. Hey, wait, you'll be taking from me. That's okay, I'll get you in the end. I always do. Thanks, mom.

  COMPONENTS ARE EATING ME ALIVE

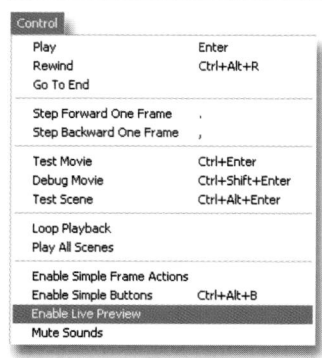

You may have noticed that when you have several compo-nents (primarily those bundled with Flash or found on MM Exchange) in any given Timeline, Flash can begin to slow down. This is due to the "Enable Live Preview" setting, which is enabled by default. When enabled, you can view how a component will look when published in the author-ing environment. Although this can be useful at times, it is not always necessary, and because having it enabled requires rendering power for every component visible on your Stage, it can slow down or annoy you on even the most powerful machines. Of course to remedy the situa-tion, simply uncheck the option by looking under Control on the menu bar. Now your components will display quickly in a draft fashion. Although this may not be the most visually appealing view, you can always switch the option back on when you need to.

   THE MISSING LINK

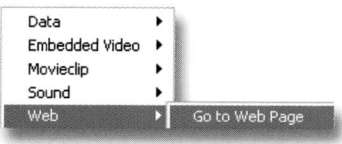

The most common question ever asked by new Flash users is, "How do I add a link in Flash that will let me jump to a specific web page?" The answer has always involved explaining the getURL action and how its parameters work. This can be rather daunting for someone who could care less about why and is just focused on getting it done.

Select any button or movie clip instance on your Stage and go to the Behaviors Panel (SHIFT-F3). From the drop-down menu, go to Web and choose "Go to web page." Now choose your target frame and URL, and Flash will automatically add the code needed to your instance. This one isn't just for newbies because it can also be a great time-saver for you seasoned pros.

FONTS FOR ALL AND FOR ALL A GOOD FONT

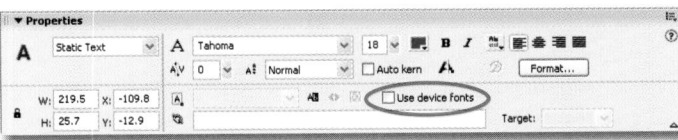

A major point of concern for any developer is making sure that everyone who views your creation sees the same exact thing.

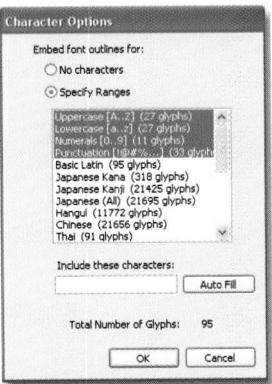

Fonts have always been a sore spot when it comes to this. The problem is that not everyone has the same set of fonts installed on their computer.

To ensure that the text in your projects is seen by everyone, select any text field. If it's a Static field, then just make sure " Use Device Fonts" is unchecked in the Property inspector. If it's Dynamic or Input, then press the Character button, choose Specify Ranges, and then select the first four items from the list. This will embed the font outlines for this font so everyone can see your text the way you do whether they have the font or not.

OLD COMPONENTS HAVE NO PLACE

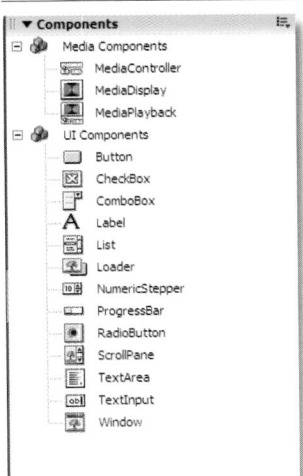

For the most part, old Flash MX components should coexist with the new 2004 components without much hassle. However, it is highly recommended that you update your old components to the new format. This is especially true if you are publishing your movie for Flash Player 7. ActionScript 2.0 seems to run into problems from time to time with the old boys.

I used a lot of the older components in my work and often tried to leave them in my new documents that I published for version 7, but I had a lot of problems. I hope things work out better for you, but if they don't, I'd say bite the bullet and spend the time updating them. Hopefully the next version of Flash won't include another major overhaul of components like the last two have. Only time will tell.

   COMPONENTS EAT UP FILE SIZE

Create a new Flash document and, without adding anything to it, publish it and check the file size of the exported SWF. It should be roughly 4K. Go back to the document and drag a button component from the Components panel onto your Stage. Re-publish your document and check the file size of the SWF again. It should be roughly 42K. I know what you're thinking: "What gives, Beav? It's only a little button!"

Go back to your document and add a Checkbox and Label component to your Stage. Check the file size again and you'll see that it only went up a few kilobytes this time. Here's the thing: Components are complex creatures and can add some considerable size to your file, but the good news is that they share a lot of the same assets when you add them. That means that the first one you add can bump your size a bit, but each one after that will share those assets and likely add very little to the size of the file.

Keep in mind that this only applies to Macromedia components or properly built components, but not necessarily all components you come across from third-party vendors.

   TRANSFORMER—MORE THAN MEETS THE EYE

There are several ways to skin a cat. There are also several ways to scale an object. Typically, you select it and use the Free Transform Tool if you just want to be able to scale freely and by sight alone. There are those out there, though, that want to be precise and exacting.

To scale any object by a percentage amount that you can type in, open your Transform panel (CTRL-T), if it's not already open. Now select the object in question. You'll see that you

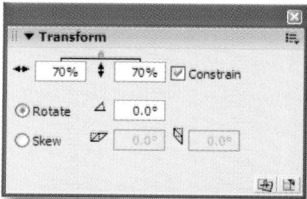

can now input precise percentages in the Transform panel to scale the object up or down at will. Check the Constrain box to make sure that the horizontal and vertical scale percentages remain proportionate. This method can be helpful if you want to make sure you have one instance that is exactly half the size of another. Using Free Transform would make it pretty hard to tell.

FLASH MEDIA PLAYER

You'll soon discover that the new components in Flash MX 2004 are extremely powerful. The ones that are built-in alone are super-handy. Take the MediaDisplay component for example. Open your Component panel (CTRL-F7 or CMD-F7) and you'll see the one I'm talking about. Drag it over to your Stage. Select the instance you created, look to the Property inspector, and you'll see a Launch Component Inspector button. Click it, and in the

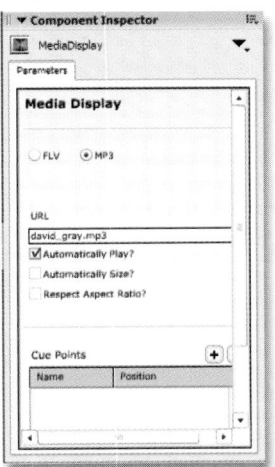 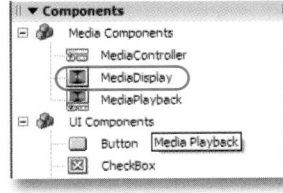

Component Inspector, choose a media type for playback (FLV or MP3) and then enter a URL (the path and filename) to load. Now, all you have to do is publish your movie and make sure that the media file you entered for the URL is in the right place.

When you run the SWF, you'll have a very nice Flash-based media player. You'll have to roll over the basic media bar in the SWF to see all the controls. Not bad, huh? Feel free to play with the other settings to see what else you can do with this cool component.

KEEP YOUR DISTANCE

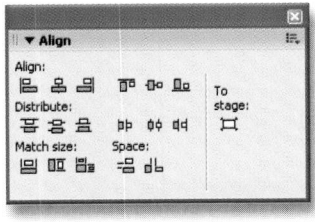

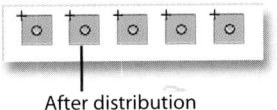

After distribution

To evenly space several objects from each other, you can sit down with paper and pencil, figure out each object's width or height, and then create a quick formula to determine the most common distance to space each object from the next. Yeah, right.

In Flash, this is known as distributing, and you can find it by opening the Align panel (CTRL-K or CMD-K on Mac). Select any number of objects on your stage and then choose from the six buttons listed under Distribute. Each option produces different results, but I'd say the one I use most often is either of the two center buttons, which will distribute evenly by center point vertically or horizontally.

All six buttons will effectively space your objects nicely and neatly, so do it any way you like it, but it certainly beats a calculator and a piece of scratch paper. Uh oh, SAT flashbacks!

   COMPONENT INSPECTOR VERSUS PROPERTY INSPECTOR

As you've seen, the Property inspector is a powerful panel that lets you set options for almost any selected item in your document. The same is true when you select a component instance. The Property inspector lists a number of options and parameters that you can set for that component.

What might seem strange is that there is also a Component inspector (ALT-F7) that lists the same parameters. Or does it? Actually, you can use the Property inspector to set the basic parameters specified by the component author. Using the Component inspector lists the basic parameters as well as several "verbose" or advanced ones for that component. Also, depending upon the component, the Component inspector may be the only place you can edit properties (i.e., MediaDisplay).

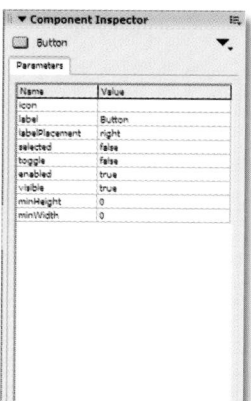

My advice is this: Always use the Property inspector unless you're a more advanced user and feel comfortable with the more advanced parameters. After all, there's really no need to have an extra panel open when one will do.

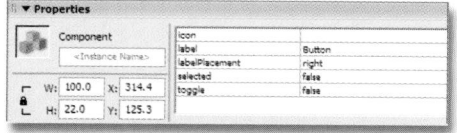

   IT'S AN EXACT SCIENCE

Careful designers who work vigorously to make sure every object's size is precise and every text field is aligned are never satisfied with positioning or sizing things with the mouse. I can't say I blame them. Sometimes there's just no substitute for perfection.

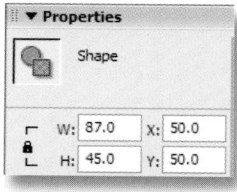

Select any object or shape on your stage and look to the Property inspector. You'll always find four properties that control the object's size and position on the stage (Width, Height, X position, Y position). You can set the exact coordinates of a text block or make sure that your logo is precisely 50x50 pixels by entering the values in these four fields.

There's even a little lock icon that, when clicked, will ensure that the Width and Height aspect ratio remains constant. Geez, the Property inspector is just so powerful, dontcha think?

GIVE A COMMAND AND FLASH WILL FOLLOW

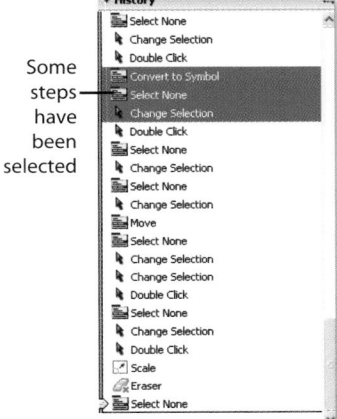

Some
steps
have
been
selected

A new feature introduced in Flash MX 2004 is the capability to save a set of actions you've performed in your document as a command that you can run at any time in the future. To turn the things you do into a command, open the new History panel (ALT-F10 or OPT-F10 on the Mac) and select the steps you want to turn into a command by clicking and dragging in the history window. Once you have the steps selected that you want, click the small disk icon at the bottom right of the panel and give your command a name. To run a saved command, look under commands and choose your command from the list. If you ever need to remove a saved command, click Manage Saved Commands in the same menu, select the command to delete and click Delete. Many of you are used to similar features in other applications such as

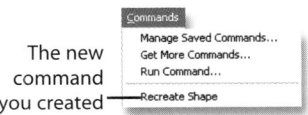

The new
command
you created

Photoshop, so I think this will be a popular option that will make redundant tasks automated and less painful.

   MOVIE EXPLORATION

With the capability to create text, movie clips, graphics, sounds, buttons, actions, and more, Flash documents can get very complex in no time. When it seems like you're losing track of things, or when you just want an outline or overview of its structure, you can use the Movie Explorer (ALT-F3 or Window > Other Panels > Movie Explorer in the menu bar, or OPT-F3 on

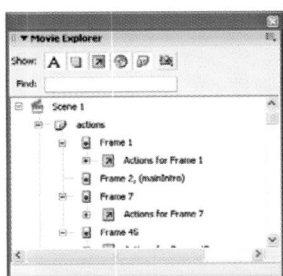

the Mac). Once open, the Movie Explorer will show you every element of your document in a flexible and easy to understand element tree. You will have the option to jump to any symbol, action, or any other elements with a simple double-click. Also, if you have specific interests such as finding a rogue empty text field, you can filter what is shown by activating the appropriate filters along the top of the Movie Explorer panel. You'll also notice a Find box that enables you to search your entire Flash document for particular keywords.

CHAPTER 8 • Tips for Built-In Components and Existing Elements   **131**

   COMMON LIBRARIES

You know those Common Libraries that come with Flash, found under Window > Other Panels > Common Libraries? Ever wish you could add your own to that list? Yeah, me too, so let's do it. These Common Libraries are just Flash documents placed in a specific directory that Flash reads. So all you have to do is create a Flash document with all the Library assets

you want frequent access to and then put it in the appropriate directory. Okay, fine, I'll tell you what directory it is. Place your document in the Libraries folder located inside the Configuration folder of your Flash application folder on your hard drive. For help, refer to the "Path to Excellence" tip in Chapter 1, "I'll Lay You Out."

It's as simple as that. There's no need to even restart Flash—your new Library is available the very next time you go to look for it. Voilà! You now have the ability to add permanent Libraries that seem to be part of Flash itself.

   SEARCH IS MY RESCUE

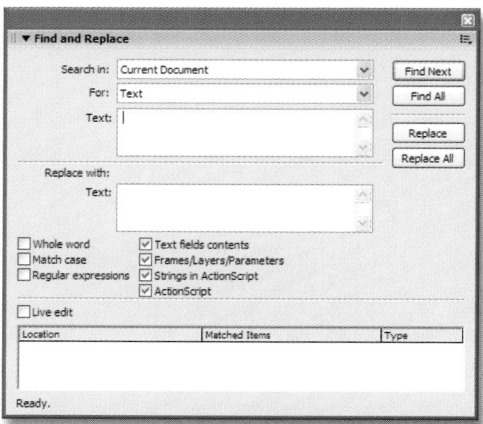

In the recent past (Flash MX), the only way to find things in your Flash document was to open the Movie Explorer panel and try to locate it in the tree. For those of you who tried this, you quickly learned that it was anything but desirable. At last Macromedia has answered our cries of despair. Pressing CTRL-F (or CMD-F on the Mac) in Flash MX 2004 will spawn a new and powerful Find and Replace window. In this window, you can search an entire document for everything from Text to Colors. The search will look through your Stage on all keyframes, as well as in your

scripts for the terms you specify. When you find the item, you can jump to it and edit it on your own, or you can let Flash do a Replace All to fix a global mistake. I think this may soon become my favorite new feature.

DEAD CENTER

Often, you may want an object to appear in the perfect horizontal and vertical center of the Stage or of a symbol. There are limitless reasons one may want to do this, but pretty much only one simple way to make it happen.

Open the Align panel by looking under Window > Design Panels or pressing CTRL-K if it isn't already available to you. Now select the object or objects on your Stage that you want to center. In the Align panel, make sure you have the "To stage:" option selected, and then press the Align Horizontal Center and Align Vertical Center buttons under the Align area of

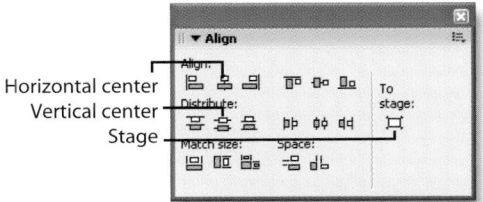

Horizontal center
Vertical center
Stage

the panel. You'll see that Flash places the registration point of the object selected dead in the center of the Stage. This can be very helpful when trying to make sure that a symbol's artwork is in the absolute center of that symbol.

   SIMPLY INTERACTIVE

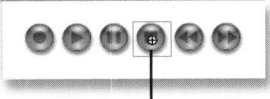

Pressing the Stop
button normally

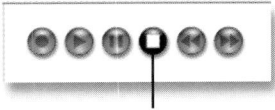

Pressing the Stop
button with Enable
Simple Buttons on

You've created some brilliantly complex Flash content and all you have to do is work out a few kinks. You may want to see what a basic button will do when you interact with it. The problem is, publishing or testing your movie can take a while.

Suffer no more. Go to Control > Enable Simple Buttons (CTRL-SHIFT-B). This will enable you to actually interact with simple buttons on your Stage as if they had been published. You can test the rollover effect as well as any sounds you may have on the button. All this without ever leaving the comfort of Flash. Keep in mind that you won't be able to move the buttons around with the mouse because they'll be responding to it. To move a button, you can either select it and move it with your arrow keys or turn this feature off and proceed as normal.

  YOUR BASIC LINEUP

Every good design tool should have the capability to line up objects and shapes at will, and Flash is no exception. To quickly align a number of objects with one another, open the Align panel by going to Window, > Design Panels, >Align (CTRL-K). Select all the objects you want to align and choose an align method under the Align area of the panel. Select Align Left, Align Horizontal Center, Align Right, Align Top, Align Vertical Center, or Align Bottom. Each of the buttons has its own way of lining things up, and they're all fairly self-explanatory.

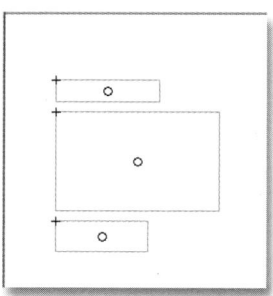 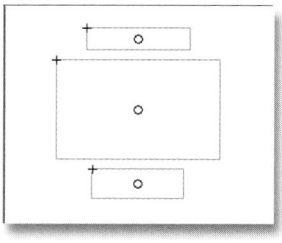 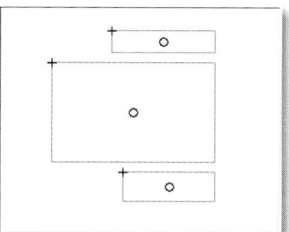

  SCENE MANAGEMENT

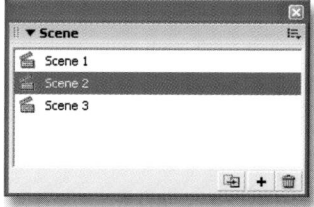

You're probably familiar with the idea of scenes by now. They can help you break your movies into sections, kind of like a slide show. Chances are, when you want to create a new scene, you go to Insert and then Scene, right? Good idea. However, there is a panel that can help you add and manage any scenes in your document. It's appropriately called the Scene panel. This panel is not included in the default layout, so you'll have to enable it yourself.

Go to Window > Design Panels > Scene (SHIFT-F2) to open the Scene panel. Here you can duplicate, add, or delete scenes using the three buttons at the bottom of the panel. You can also jump to a scene by double-clicking one of the scenes listed. If you're big on scenes, this panel will be your new friend. At least until it steals money from you.

   QUICK BUGS OR DEBUGS?

Any way you look at it, we all experience times when our code just isn't doing what we think it should. Right? Okay, maybe I'm the only one, but if not, check this out. Flash comes with a rather robust Debugger window to help developers solve their movie problems (mostly ActionScripters).

A quick way to have the Debugger appear when the time is right is by going to the Control menu and choosing Debug Movie (CTRL-SHIFT-ENTER or SHIFT-CMD-RETURN on Mac). This is very much like the commonly used Test Movie, but with one exception—debugging is auto-

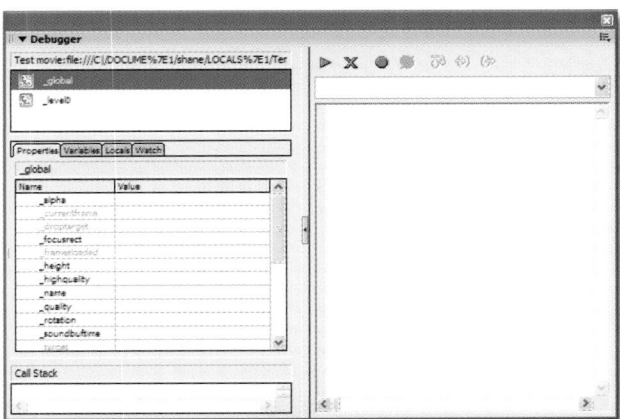

matically enabled and the Debugger window appears while your movie is being tested as a published SWF.

Debugging can be a rather complex process, and because this is merely a tip book, I won't go into the thousands of ways one should use the Debugger. Maybe if you tell me how much you love this book, I'll write another one that goes even further.

    I'M LOOPY

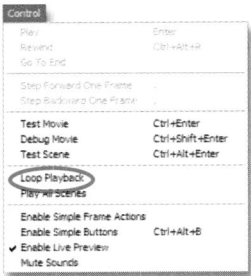

You're all well aware of the fact that Flash movie Timelines will loop by default, right? This is very true if you've published your movie as a SWF and you're watching your animation in the player. However, if you're just playing through the Timeline while working in the authoring environment, you'll see that there is no looping. Instead, the play head reaches the end of the Timeline and stops.

If you like the loopy playback, there's a simple solution. Instead of testing your movie to see it loop, you can go to the Control menu and click Loop Playback. Now press Enter or play in any Timeline and it will loop as if you had published it. You can toggle this option to suit your needs, but it's just nice knowing it's there.

  UNGROUP OR BREAK APART?

Many of us use grouping to move or categorize multiple objects on the Stage as one larger object or group. This adds less size to a movie than creating a symbol, and it's best to use this when you don't have objects that are used over and over.

When you group several objects using CTRL-G or CMD–G on the Mac, you can select that group in the future and go to Modify > Ungroup (CTRL-SHIFT-G or SHIFT-CMD–G on the Mac) to remove the grouping and return all the items to their normal individual state. What I never understood is that you can select a group and press CTRL-B or CMD-B to break apart the group, and it has the same exact effect. So the question is, "Why use one over the other?" Well, there is no reason, so I say always use CTRL-B. You don't have to remember another key combo, and you save yourself having to hold down a third key. Wow, I just realized how lazy I am.

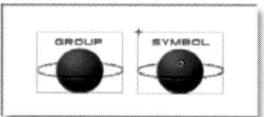 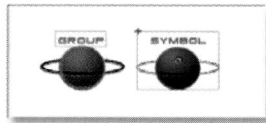 

| After ungrouping both objects | After breaking apart both objects |

  FONT MAPPING

Any time I work in with a team of developers on a Flash project, I always run into one particular problem. When I open someone else's FLA files, I get a message saying that I don't have some freaky font they decided to use in their design. The cool thing is that Flash picks up on this and gives me an option to pick a font I do have to use until I get and install the weird font.

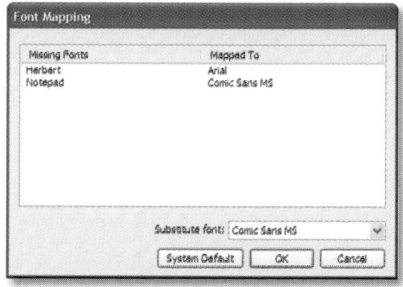

Ideally, you want to pick a substitute that is close to the font you're missing, but you may not get this on the first try. If you ever decide to switch to another substitute, just go to Edit > Font Mappings (Flash MX > Font Mappings on Mac) and select a new font for the missing one. It may take some trial and error if you don't know what the missing font looks like, but eventually you'll find something that seems to fit.

SPELL CHECKER?

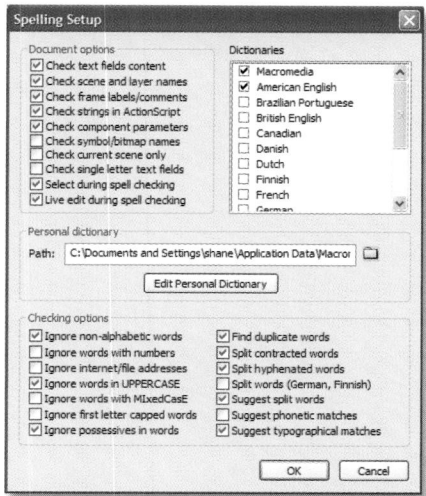

I'm not talking about someone who checks to make sure you cast your spell properly. I know that's the first thing that came to your mind, but no. Flash MX 2004 comes with a rather powerful and long-overdue spell-checking function. Before you go rushing to spellcheck every old document you have, you'll need to set up the function first. Go to Text, > Spelling Setup. Here you can choose from several options that will tell Flash what and how to spell-check in your documents. Click OK to tell Flash you're happy with the settings, return to the Text menu, and choose Check Spelling to run the new tool. You can even edit misspellings without leaving the spell-check window. Oh, and you can go back to Spelling Setup at any time to alter your settings, but you probably already knew that.

HELP, I NEED SOMEBODY... HELP

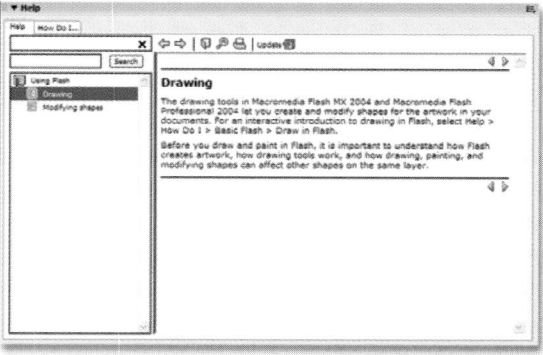

If you're a long-time user of Flash, then you may remember what it was like when you had to update your help files. In the past, the Flash help system was a series of HTML pages, and an entire updated set of pages was released at one point to correct mistakes and add new information. With Flash MX 2004, the help system is integrated in the Flash interface, and there's even a nifty auto-update feature.

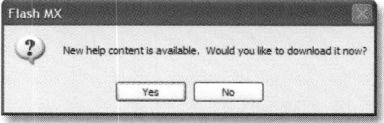

In the Help panel, click the Update button to automatically download any changes or additions Macromedia may have made to the help system. Now if they'd only include an auto-update link for Flash itself.

CHAPTER 8 • Tips for Built-In Components and Existing Elements   **137**

  ICONS FOR ALL

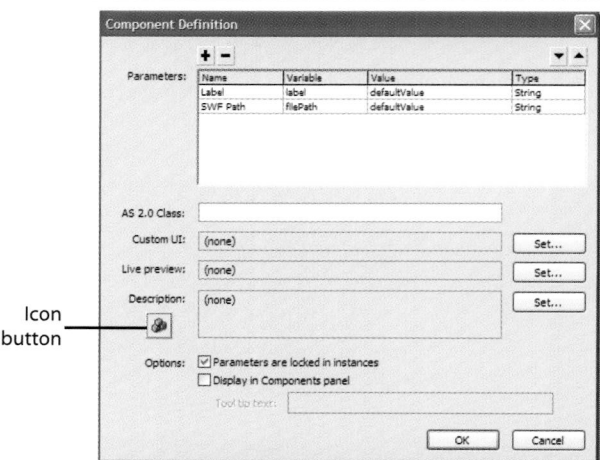

Icon
button

Some of you have ventured into the brave world of creating your own components. Beginning with Flash MX, components have provided us with a wonderful way to make reusable and customizable code. You may have noticed that every time you made one of these components, the only thing that distinguished one from the other in the Library was the name. They always seem to have the same boring icon (three colored cubes).

To add a little flavor to your component, right-click it in the Library and choose Component Definition. In the window that appears, click the typical three-cubed icon, which is actually a button. This will provide you with a drop-down list of available icons for your component. You're still a little limited, but at least they won't all look the same.

   SHARE AND SHARE ALIKE

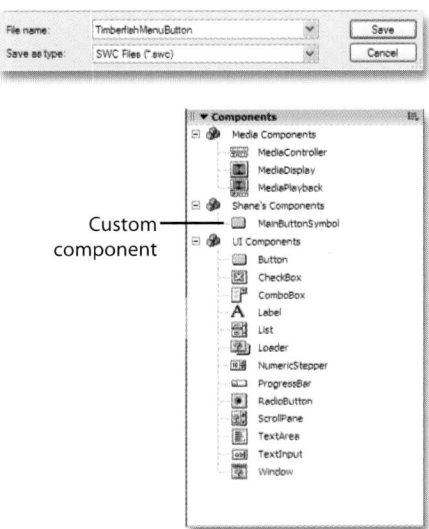

Custom component

If you are one of those people who love to create your own components and then distribute them to friends or co-workers, Flash MX 2004 makes this a really easy process.

Right-click on your component in your Library and choose Export SWC File. Give your file a name and then place the file in your Configuration\Components folder. For the exact location of this folder for your operating system, look at the "Common Libraries" tip earlier in this chapter. Now moving on… Look to the panel menu at the top right and choose Reload. You'll see your own component listed in the Components panel (CTRL-F7), alongside all those cool built-in components you've been looking at all this time.

   JUST THE ONES YOU WANT

As mentioned in the tip "Share and Share Alike," you can easily add your own components to the Components panel (CTRL-F7) and access them at will without having to load them manually. The great thing about the Components panel is that it lists any and all components that are placed in a particular directory and even organizes them based on any folders you put in that directory. Go to the Configuration\Components folder. For the exact location of this folder for your operating system, look at the "Common Libraries" tip. Once you find the Components folder, you'll see three sub-folders inside. Each one contains a list of SWC files (compiled components). If you know you'll never use some of them, you can move them to another folder for safe-keeping so that they don't clutter your panel.

Of course, this means you can add any components you've picked up and even organize them in your own folders, which will be reflected in the panel. When you're done making changes, just go to the panel menu of the Components panel and choose Reload. This will update the panel with the changes you've made. Love it!

It's Not Sanskrit

ActionScript Tips

Wanna hear a funny story? Me neither, so I'll tell this one instead. When I first encountered ActionScript, I thought the guy said "Sanskrit." Being the dedicated

It's Not Sanskrit
Tips for ActionScript

professional I am (that was funny), I signed up for a two-year intensive course in Egypt to learn the ancient written language of pictures. I returned from my long journey with the ability to decipher third-dynasty Egyptian hieroglyphics. I felt prepared to take on the entire Flash world. Of course, then I found out that the guy said "ActionScript" and discovered that I was right back where I started. Now some people say that I'm an idiot for my mistake, but I like to think of it as a creative misinterpretation of the English language. Besides, I can now read/write in a three-thousand year-old language, which is a great conversation piece in groups. From the little I actually do know about ActionScript, I'll say that this chapter covers a lot of the popular tasks one might use it for. If you're like me and you don't know much about this crazy language, then I think you'll like this chapter and what it can do to fill out your toolset. Just remember…it's not Sanskrit. It'll save you a couple years.

DRAG 'N DROP CODING?

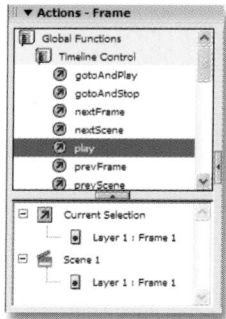

When Flash 5 was released, ActionScript received its first major makeover, which took away the capability to apply scripts using drop-downs or drag-and-drop methods. This made some people very happy, while others were just freaked out. Luckily, the Actions panel always had the Normal mode setting for those who didn't know how or didn't want to deal with typing their code by hand. For you guys, there's bad news and good news. The bad news is that there is no more Normal mode for Flash MX 2004. The good news is that you can still drag and drop code.

Open the Actions panel and make sure the left frame of the panel is expanded to reveal a list of predefined actions. Now drag the desired action over to the script pane. You can also double-click

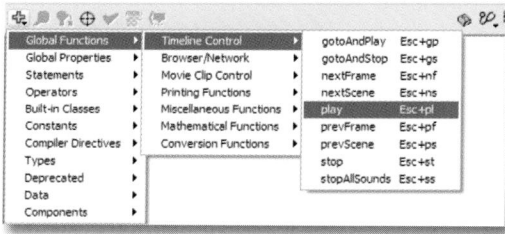

the action to get the same result. If you need a slightly faster solution, you can always go to the + button at the top left of the Script pane of the Actions panel where you'll get the same list of actions in a menu style. Make sure that you have your cursor in the location you want the script to appear when adding any action this way.

EXTERNALIZE ACTIONSCRIPT

Let's say you have several lengthy scripts that you use in multiple Flash documents. Updating them can be a hassle because you have to open each file, locate the script, and make the changes. Here's a way you can actually keep all your nifty scripts in their own documents and never actually place them in Flash. Doing this will let you create your own library of scripts, share them as you like, and make changes to one location when necessary. To do that, either copy and paste an existing script or write a new one into a text file and save it with a .as extension. You can now put the following line of code on a keyframe in your document.

```
#include "yourfilenamehere.as"
```

Flash will automatically load the script from your file each time it's published, tested, or exported. And guess what—you can also edit .as files with your favorite text editor or Dreamweaver MX 2004, which will provide AS syntax highlighting and code hints.

   ## I'M GETTING NEW HIGHLIGHTS

If you've done any programming in other environments such as Visual Studio.NET, you may be used to a specific kind of color highlighting in your code. ActionScript 2.0 comes with highlighting of its own, using colors unique to Flash of course. However, you can easily change these highlighting colors to closely match other environments to which you may be accustomed. Open your Preferences window using CTRL-U (or Flash > Preferences on the Mac) and switch to the ActionScript tab. Under Syntax coloring, you'll be able to set highlighting colors for six different parts of the Actions panel. I for one don't like that Identifiers and Keywords are the same color by default, so I usually change one of the two for distinction. Ah lovely, just one more way to totally customize your Flash environment.

   ## WHAT LINE IS THAT?

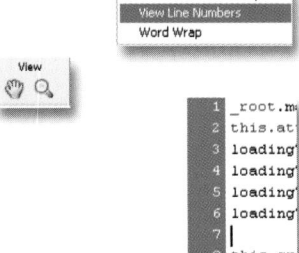

Okay, this one is more for the people out there who frequently write their own ActionScript or have long scripts in their documents. Say you publish your document, only to get some vague error in the Output window referring to a line number for your script. Okay, great, now I have to scroll down using my arrow key and watch the little text at the bottom of my Actions panel indicating what line I'm on. Not true! Go to the View Options menu, which looks like a little blue arrow at the top right of the Actions panel, and select View Line Numbers from the drop-down. Hey, that's much better! Now all you have to do is use the scrollbar to go down to the line that's giving you trouble. This feature could also come in handy if you're bragging to your friends about how many lines of code you wrote. Wait, more is better, right?

HINT, HINT…

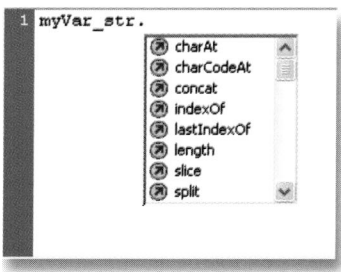

When using the ActionScript window, Flash has automatic completion support, which means that as you type, a list of methods and properties for known code will appear. You may have already noticed that while typing `_root`, Flash automatically gives you a list of actions that apply to a movie clip. The cool thing is that Flash will do this for your own customized variables too. However, because Flash doesn't keep track of what type your variable is, you'll have to name them according to a specific format in order to take advantage of this built-in tip system. The trick is to suffix the name of your variable with a couple letters that indicate to Flash what type of variable you are referring to. Then Flash will pop up a list of actions and methods for that type of object even though it's your own variable and one that's built into Flash. Some of the most commonly used suffixes are listed below. Name your variables with these suffixes and Flash will make typing code easier than ever and make your code easier for others to follow and understand. For a complete list of supported suffixes, search Flash's help system for "triggers code hints" and you'll see them all.

Type	Suffix	Example
Array	_array	myList_array
Button	_btn	myButton_btn
Color	_color	myColor_color
Date	_date	myDate_date
Movie Clip	_mc	myMovie_mc
Sound	_sound	myMusic_sound
String	_str	myVar_str
Text Field	_txt	myField_txt
XML	_xml	myData_xml

RIGHT-CLICK NO MORE

By default, right-clicking on any Flash movie will bring up a list of options for the person viewing it. They can Zoom, Print, and even control the playback of your movie. In Flash MX, the only way around this was to set a special parameter in the HTML that contained your Flash movie to disable the right-click menu.

With the release of Flash MX 2004, there is a new AS object called `ContextMenu` that enables you to have control over that same right-click menu. Add the following code to the first keyframe in your main Timeline, publish your movie, and right-click on it to see what happens.

```
var newMenu = new ContextMenu();
newMenu.hideBuiltInItems();
_root.menu = newMenu;
```

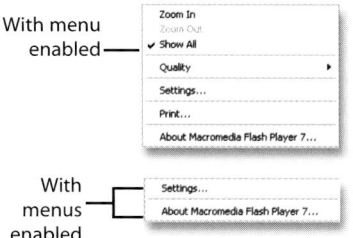

With menu enabled

With menus enabled

You'll see that all right-click options have been disabled, and the user only gets the Settings and About options when the menu appears. These two remaining options cannot be hidden because they control a user's plug-in settings and give information about the version.

   I'M IGNORING YOU NOW

Dealing with XML in Flash isn't always the easiest thing to do. There are just so many darn rules. For one, if you're importing an XML file into an XML object and your file was created with tabs, spaces, and return characters in it (as most are), then you can run into some trouble. Flash will treat these characters (known as white space) as if they are nodes themselves, and that can cause big problems. You could just remove all the white space and make the file one long string, but that's hard to read. Instead, just use this code.

```
myData = new XML();
myData.ignoreWhite = true;
myData.load("myfile.xml");
```

With the `ignoreWhite` attribute set to `true`, Flash will simply ignore those pesky characters and treat the entire file as if it were one long string of text. It seems to me that `ignoreWhite` should be set to `true` by default, but that's just me.

CHAPTER 9 • Tips for ActionScript   **145**

   CALLING ALL JAVASCRIPT!

At first, you may think that calling a JavaScript function from Flash is difficult, but it's really not. Knowing JavaScript itself is going to be the hardest part about this tip. If you have a JavaScript function defined on the same HTML page where your Flash movie is embedded, then all you have to do is put the following code in your document.

On a button or movie clip instance:

```
on(release) {
   getURL("javascript:myFunction();");
}
```

On a keyframe (frame action):

```
getURL("javascript:myFunction();");
```

It's actually the same concept as targeting an HTML page, except you put `"javascript:"` followed by the function you're calling where the URL would be.

   CREATE EMAIL

A very common question that many people have about Flash is, "How can I create an email using Flash?" The truth is, you can't. But Flash can make an HTML call that will open a new email message. This is assuming that the user has an email client installed on his/her machine.

On a button or movie clip instance:

```
on(release) {
   getURL("mailto:email@domainname.com");
}
```

On a keyframe (frame action):

```
getURL("mailto:email@domainname.com");
```

Adding the `mailto:` directive will automatically open a new email message on the user's machine. If the person does not have an email client or their client is not configured correctly, this method can fail. However, this is a very common method used in HTML, and it's typically very reliable.

LOOPY LOU

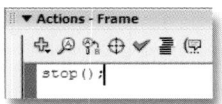

I'm sure you noticed that by default the main Timeline of your Flash movie will loop over and over again until you do something to stop it. The same is true for any movie clip symbol's Timeline. I don't know about you, but I want my clips to play one time and stop. If you're like me and all this looping drives you loopy, then try this. Go to the Timeline you want to keep from looping. Create a new layer and name it **actions** if you don't already have one there. Go to the very last frame of that Timeline and create a keyframe on your actions layer. Open the Actions panel (F9) and select that last keyframe. Type `stop();` into the Actions panel. Now when this Timeline is being played back, it will reach the end, find your simple stop action, and do just that.

YOU'VE BEEN PINNED

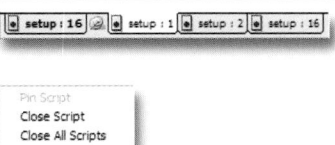

Hardcore developers often find the Flash Actions panel a bit limited when it comes to working with complex scripts. A lot has changed in MX 2004 to make things easier for the developer, and one of them is the capability to view multiple scripts at once.

Start by viewing any script in the Actions panel. At the bottom of the panel, click the pin icon to make that script stick to the Actions panel. Now you can go to any other location in your document, view other scripts, and pin them too. This will give you quick access to a number of scripts throughout your document, all of which are accessible with one click of a tab. To close a pinned script, activate it and click the pin icon again.

If you need to close all pinned scripts at once, you can right-click any script tab and choose Close All Scripts. I don't know about you, but when I found this one, I was thrilled considering how much time I waste jumping from script to script and having to hunt each one down.

  IGNORE THIS CODE

I think it's wise to write code (ActionScript) that Flash pays attention to, but there are certain reasons you would want code to be ignored. This is referred to in programming circles as "commenting out code." There are two ways to comment out code in ActionScript. The first way lets you comment out a single line of code; it's done like this:

```
// Anything I type on this line will be ignored by Flash
```

The second way enables you to define a start point (/*) and end point (*/) for your commented code, and it can cover many lines:

```
/* Nothing on any of these
lines will be compiled by
Flash's ActionScript engine so I can write
whatever I want. */
```

You can use either method to disable code for testing, to add a note about the code, or just to save your grocery list, and it will be ignored. All commented code is shaded in gray by default.

   AUTO FORMAT

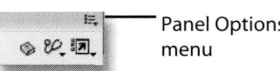

Panel Options menu

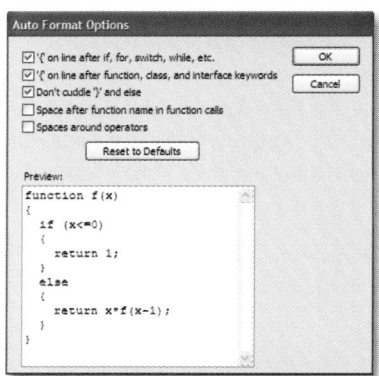

Attention programmers, this one's for you! If you're used to working with Visual Studio, Borland Products, or even IBM software, you may be used to your code formatting itself a certain way as you type. Working in Flash can be a bit different, and the code you write can feel funny because it just isn't the same. Don't give up yet. Open the Actions Panel Options menu and choose Auto Format Options from the list. Here, you'll be able to tinker with the way ActionScript is formatted so that the code you write looks more like what you're used to. I typically keep the first three options checked because I'm used to working in Visual Studio .NET. You even get a little preview of how your code will look when you accept the formatting options.

POP IT RIGHT

Even though this tip has a lot to do with JavaScript, it is one of the most common questions asked of me. "How do I pop up a new window in Flash with no border, buttons, menu, etc…?" Okay, calling JavaScript functions from Flash was discussed earlier in the "Calling All JavaScript!" tip, so now I'll build on that a little. First add the code to call the JavaScript somewhere using this command:

```
getURL("javascript:myPopup('http://www.mydomain.com');");
```

Now add this JavaScript code in between the `<head>` `</head>` tags in the HTML page that the Flash movie will be placed in.

```
<script language="JavaScript" type="text/JavaScript">
<!--
function myPopup(url)
{
  window.open(url,"newWin","width=500, height=500");
}
//-->
</script>
```

You can change the width and height values in the JavaScript to whatever pixel value you want for your new window. If you need more customized options for the new window, you may want to look into the `window.open` command in JavaScript, but for the basic pop-up, this is simple and clean. You can also forgo putting JavaScript on the page and just call the window.open function in the getURL instead of calling myPopup.

 LOCK THE ROOT

Let's say you have a movie called Main.fla, which loads several Flash movies (SWF files) into it while it runs using the loadMovie command. One of these files is Footer.swf, and in Footer.swf you have a lot of code that refers to `_root`. If you run Footer.swf on its own, the code will run fine because `_root` refers to the main Timeline of Footer.swf. However, once you've loaded Footer.swf into Main.swf, `_root` will point to the Main.swf Timeline.

There are many of you that have had to deal with this little quirk over and over. With Flash MX 2004, there is a new Boolean variable called `_lockroot` that corrects this issue. Place the following code in the Footer.fla main Timeline:

```
this._lockroot = true;
```

Now, referring to `_root` in Footer.swf will actually point to the main Timeline of Footer.swf, even when it has been loaded into another movie. I don't know about you, but this is one of my favorites!

   I'M JUST NOT READY

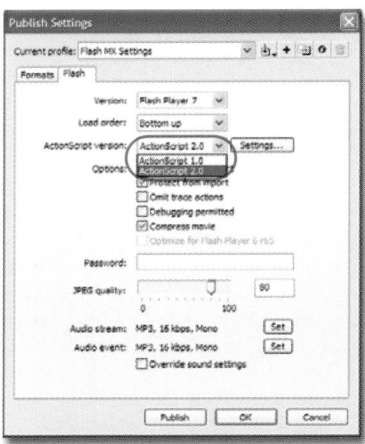

A lot of people (especially non-programmers) are still playing catch up when it comes to learning ActionScript. So I'm sure most of them were very pleased to hear that ActionScript got a major upgrade to version 2.0.

Don't worry, though. If you want to transition to the new version slowly over time, that's your decision to make. Open your Publish Settings for any Flash document (CTRL-SHIFT-F12), go to the Flash tab, and you'll see the option to publish your movie using good ol' AS 1.0.

If you choose to do this for a while, I would still recommend learning how to use AS 2.0 effectively. Eventually, version 1 will be deprecated, and it's only a matter of time before everyone will be using version 2, and you don't want to be different, do you? Do you?!

   SCROLLABLE TEXT

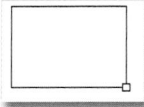

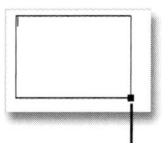

After holding SHIFT and double-clicking handle to make scrollable

Let's make a scrollable text field in about one minute, whaddya say? First, create a dynamic text field by using the Text Tool to click and drag a rectangular field. Now, hold SHIFT while you double-click the white square handle on the text field (this quickly sets the field to scrollable—doing it again would turn scrollable off). Give your text field an instance name (I'm using `scrollText`). Now place any two buttons to represent the up and down scroll arrows. Select the up button, go to the Actions panel, and place the following code there....

```
on(release)
{
        scrollText.scroll -= 1;
}
```

Do the same for the down button, but change the -= to +=. True, it seems like it would be the opposite, but the += will move the text up, which makes the text appear to be scrolling down. Now, just enter a lot of text in the field, and you're done. You could also set the text dynamically using ActionScript if you're so inclined. A quick, dirty, and lovely little tool to add to your belt.

HERE'S A HINT

Code Hints are a helpful tool when you're writing ActionScript. It's very difficult to remember the exact names of all properties and methods for every code object in the language. However, if automatic hints annoy you sometimes, or you'd rather just call on them when you need them, then turn 'em off.

In the Preferences panel (CTRL-U) under the ActionScript tab, deselect the Code Hints option. You can still call on these hints when you need them by pressing the Show Code Hint button (CTRL-Spacebar) in the Actions panel to manually display them. They just aren't going to insult you by anticipating that you need help every time you place a "." in your Actions.

LOADMOVIE DOESN'T LOAD A JPEG

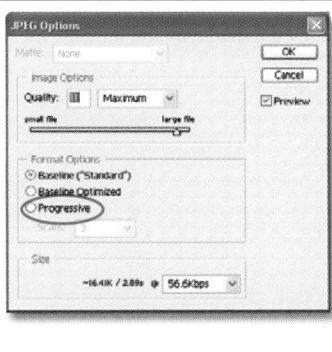

If you've moved into the more advanced world of Flash development, then you've no doubt attempted to load a JPEG image into your SWF using the `loadMovie` command. When they introduced this capability, I was thrilled. No more converting to SWFs! However, you may have run into some trouble with certain JPEGs not loading. Do you want to know why? Chances are, the image in question is set to be progressive. A progressive JPEG is one that can be viewed in a browser as it loads. The problem is that the Flash player does not have a compressor for progressive JPEGs like the Flash authoring program does. It's a good idea to constantly test your movies to make sure that your images are loading as expected. If you find one that is not, chances are good that this is the reason. Convert the image to a non-progressive JPEG, and you're all set.

   SUDDENLY SENSITIVE

You may have noticed that a lot of your ActionScript code started breaking when you put it in Flash MX 2004. There are a lot of changes that were made, and if you want to convert your code to the new AS 2.0 format, it will take some work. One big change is the fact that in AS 2.0, identifiers (instance names, variables) are now case-sensitive. That means that while you could use `myVar` and `MyVar` interchangeably in previous versions of Flash, now they are treated as two completely different identifiers.

This may take some getting used to for some of you, but believe me, it's much better this way. I would recommend always paying close attention to text case when doing any scripting or programming, whether the language demands it or not. I always said that they would make ActionScript case-sensitive one day, but did people listen? Well, actually, yes, a lot of them did, so never mind.

   I HAVE A COMMENT

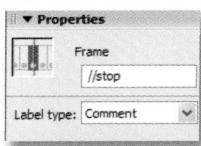 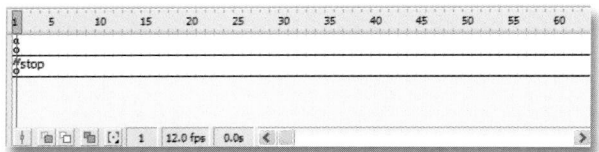

It's common practice to place comments throughout your ActionScript to keep track of changes or make notes about the code, but who ever heard of putting a comment on a frame in the Timeline? Trust me, they're useful. For example, let's say you have a simple stop action on your Timeline, but you keep forgetting what actions are on that frame because all you see is a little "a" above the keyframe. Instead of continually selecting the frame to see what's there, you can add a comment to remind yourself.

Select any keyframe, look to the Property inspector, and type a comment ("stop" in this case) into the Frame Label field. Now change the label type to Comment. Flash will ignore the comment, but you'll be easily reminded of what kind of code you put there. You can use these comments for a number of reasons, so long as you use them. They help others understand what's going on in your Timeline, and doing this forces them to take you out for dinner after work. I promise.

You can accomplish the same effect a bit quicker by just creating a frame label and putting "//" in front of the name you give it.

DO NOT PRINT

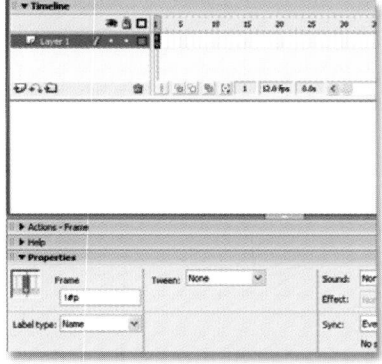

Whenever someone watches your movie in a browser, they can right-click any part of your movie and get some options. One of those options enables them to print all the frames in your main Timeline with a single click. Often, this is not something you want to let them do, especially if you're trying to protect any visual content.

To prevent this, create a label on the first frame of your main Timeline with the name ! #p as shown. This will prevent anyone from printing your Timeline without having to go through the trouble of disabling menu items. Those of you who are big on copy protection should really enjoy this one.

   TRACE AN ACTION

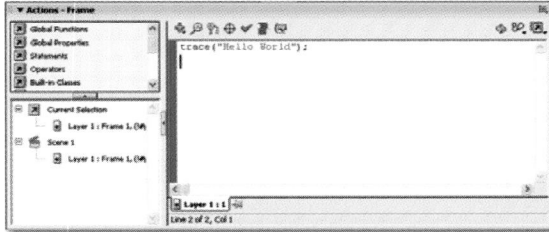

A lot of times I run into an issue where my script won't work. I examine it, only to find no problems whatsoever. Or so it seems. The problem is that when you are the only one looking at your work and you've been staring at it for hours, it can be difficult to identify problems. Usually I find that I've done something really stupid, like misspelling a variable name.

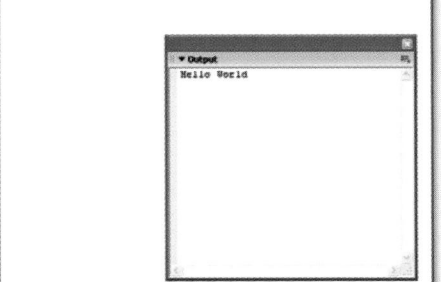

One of the things that can quickly help you identify where a problem lies is the trace action. Add it at any place in your script, like this:

```
trace("Hello World");
```

Now test your movie using CTRL-ENTER (or CMD-ENTER) and you'll see a new Output window appear with the words Hello World. Basically anything you put in the parentheses of a trace

action will print to the Output window, whether it be a variable or a string value as we used previously. This can be very helpful to give you some immediate feedback or output to test your scripts.

   BEST WAY TO HIDE USER MENU

One very popular thing that developers do is disable the menu that users are shown when they right-click any Flash content that appears in their browser. We already discussed Flash MX 2004's new way of accomplishing this, but the classic way is still the best.

In the code of the HTML page in which your Flash movie is embedded, you'll see an `<object>` tag and an `<embed>` tag. These two tags work together so that Flash will be properly displayed in IE and non-IE browsers alike. To hide the right-click menu options for a movie, add the following param tag to the object tag of the HTML page.

```
<param name="menu" value="false">
```

Now add the menu parameter to the embed tag anywhere in the list of parameters already there.

```
menu="false"
```

Sure, the new Flash player enables you to do this using ActionScript, but the method above will work for many older Flash player versions as well. So if you're still publishing Flash 6 content, you can still do a happy little dance. Well, you can do that anyway.

   GOING LOCAL

I noticed that a large number of people have the desire to load an SWF or other file into their Flash movie from a local drive. Perhaps they want to link to a file that they know will be on a user's hard drive or want to load an image with `loadMovie` that they know will be on a local drive. There's a right and a wrong way to do this. I see no point in telling you the wrong way, so just take a look at the right way next.

Any time you refer to a file on a local machine and you know its absolute path (location), make sure you place this in front of the path to the file. Think of it as `http://` but intended for the local computer.

```
file://
```

This code refers to the computer that is running the Flash movie. So, opening an image called `alwaysthere.jpg` on the C drive would look like this:

```
_root.loadMovie("file://c/alwaysthere.jpg");
```

BUTTON ACTIONS WORKED IN THE OLD DAYS, SO WHAT'S UP?

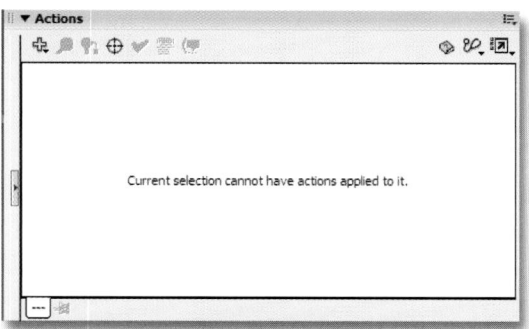

Current selection cannot have actions applied to it.

In the past, designers would often place frame actions on a button's timeline. While this method worked, it was certainly not recommended. Don't feel bad if you did (or do) this because I did it myself long ago. If you're doing it now, stop because Flash MX 2004 no longer allows it. In fact, if you select a frame on a button's timeline and then go to the Actions panel, you'll find a message instead of a place to put an action. The proper place to put a button action is on the instance itself. Select a button instance and place your actions there. Dontcha' hate it when they start enforcing rules that were never enforced before?

Let's Get Embed

Movin' the Flash Movie

Look, I've put you all through quite a bit by now. All of the other introductions and most of my tips have been blanketed in wise cracks and witty anecdotes.

Let's Get Embed

Tips for Placing Your Flash Movie on Your Site

I have no intention of putting you through any more of that. Instead let me give you a brief overview of post-war Iraq. Oops, there I go again. Okay, the chapter… This final chapter is full of what I think are the most valuable tips of them all. These are the ones that can truly separate the men from the boys in the Flash design community. Everyone may be able to make Flash movies, but only a few of us can do it right and make our animations as efficient as possible. After you read this chapter and commit every word to memory, you'll be on your way to elevating yourself to that upper echelon of designer. Congratulations on your new promotion, but most of all give yourself a pat on the back for finding this book. Oh, and thank you for your contribution to my ongoing and very expensive psychotherapy.

   ## ESTIMATED PERFORMANCE

You may develop most of your Flash movies for 56K users, while being on a DSL or other high-speed connection yourself. This makes testing your movies for slower connections difficult. To test how your movie will perform under various situations, test your movie using CTRL-ENTER and then select Bandwidth Profiler from the View menu. What you'll see is a graph displaying how much data is sent for each frame of your movie according to various modem speeds you specify. If you set the modem speed under Download Settings in the View menu to 56K, you'll be able to get information simulating a user on a 56K modem.

Each bar of the graph represents a frame of your movie. If any frame goes above the red line, you know that the user will have to wait for that frame to load. You can change the Download Setting speed to test different connections and see where your movie needs optimizing. This is a very useful tool when you're optimizing your movie for slow connection speeds.

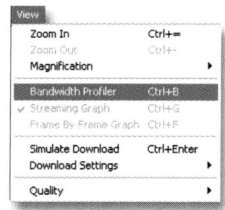 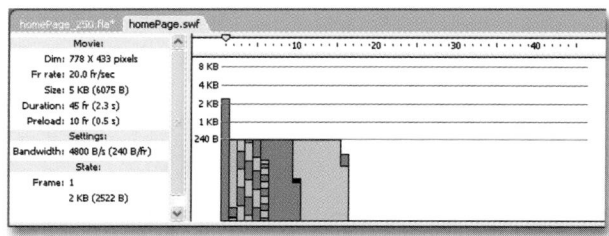

  ## OUTLAWED OUTLINES

In most cases when you embed your fonts as previously mentioned, you'll want to embed all possible characters for that font, just in case you need to use them all. However, if you're sure

that you only need certain characters, then you can often significantly reduce your file size by including only the ones you need. Let's say you have a dynamic field that will only display numbers. There's no need to embed outlines for every letter in the alphabet, so don't. Select the text field, bring up the Character Options again, and this time only select the Numerals set from the list. Doing this throughout your movie can be a great way to cut down on file size. Keep in mind that if you have two text fields (Dynamic or Input) of the same font and one only has Numeric included while the other has all outlines, you won't save any space. If they're included for one field, then they're in your final SWF file, so do this only when it can actually make a difference.

   TRANSPARENT SWFS?

Normally, the world of transparent backgrounds is only reserved for GIF images on HTML pages. However, Flash has a rarely-used feature that will enable your movies to have a transparent background too.

Go to Publish Settings (CTRL-SHIFT-F12) and on the HTML tab, change the Window Mode to Transparent Windowless. Publish your document and make a few changes to the published HTML page so that your page has a background image or something else that will be different from the standard background.

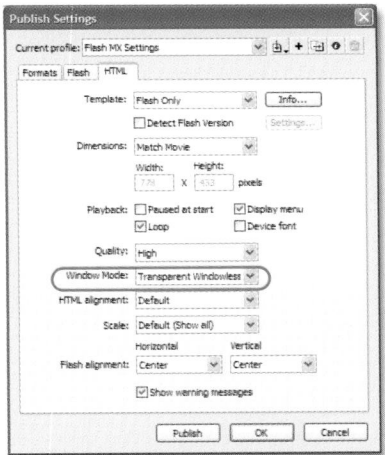

If you have Flash in an existing HTML page, add the following parameter to the OBJECT tag:

```
<param name=" wmode" value="transparent">
```

Add the following parameter to the EMBED tag:

```
wmode=" transparent"
```

Macromedia Flash Player version 6,0,65,0 (Windows) or 6,0,67,0 (Macintosh) or higher and a compatible browser are required for this feature to work. You should check www.macromedia.com for an up-to-date list of compatible browsers because the list will change in the future. Despite the minor restrictions, this tip can make for some very cool overlapping of HTML and Flash content.

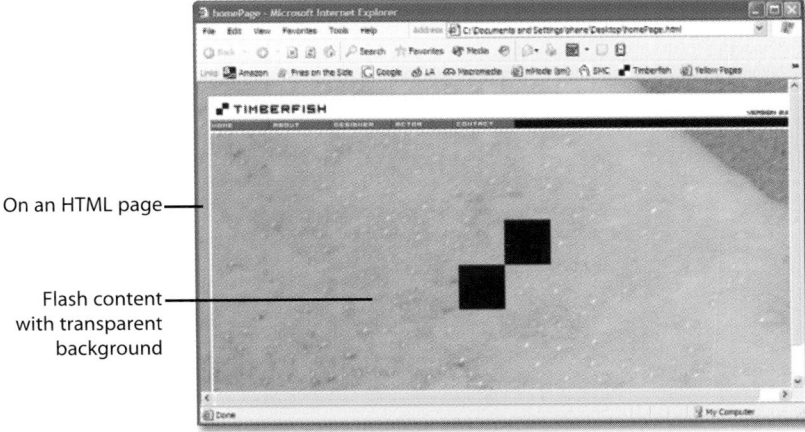

On an HTML page——

Flash content—— with transparent background

   WEB SAFE HAS CHANGED

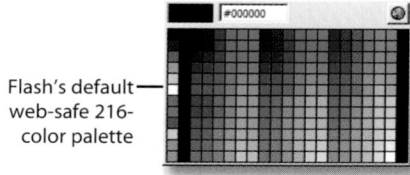

Flash's default web-safe 216-color palette

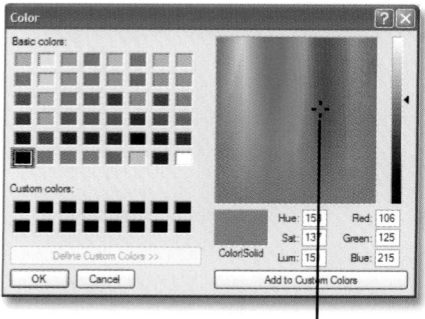

Use Custom Color button to make your own custom color

One of the givens of web design is that you must only use a color that's in the web-safe 216-color palette. Only a few short years ago, most computers had basic video cards that only supported 8 bits of color (256 colors). Then it was discovered that to make sure all designs looked the same on Netscape, IE, Macs, and PCs, people had to use a basic set of common colors that worked for all. These colors are the 216 colors that became known as "web safe." If you use these colors, your designs will be viewed the same by everyone on the Net. The problem is that these colors suck, and a majority (94%) of today's monitors are set to display millions of colors. So, it's my recommendation that you open your mind and forget about the standard 216 rule. Flash clings to this palette by setting it as the default. Don't be afraid to create your own custom colors.

   RESIZING ACCORDINGLY

Any time you are absolutely unsure about what size to make your Flash movie, you can try to create all your artwork first and then crop it down. Unfortunately, cropping in Flash isn't as easy as it is in Photoshop or Fireworks, so you have to keep one thing in mind. Do your best to keep your content in the upper-left corner of the Stage because any time you resize your document, it simply shaves off or adds to the bottom and right edges of the stage.

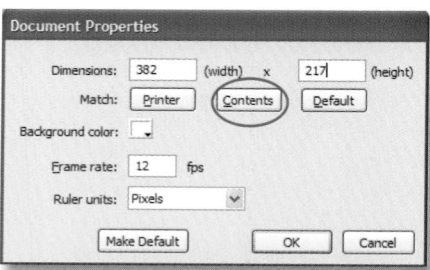

Now, the nifty part of the process is that when you're done with your work, you can open Document Properties (CTRL-J or CMD-J) and press the Contents button. This will automatically resize your document to match what you have on the Stage and leave a little margin just in case. Maybe cropping will become easier one day, but for now, it's Match Contents.

    DOCUMENT SIZES

When you create a new Flash document, the movie size is always set to a default size of 550¥400 pixels. It may seem like an arbitrary size, but it actually makes sense. The most common screen size used to be 640¥480, and if you're looking at Flash in a browser, many pixels are taken up by the browser window itself. Setting the movie to 550¥400 made certain that everyone could see your entire movie. Now the more common screen size is 800¥600, which will soon be replaced by yet a larger size. So asking "What size should I make my movies?" is a great question. The answer is that there is no single answer. You'll want to ask yourself the following questions first: "What will my movie be? A button, a toolbar, an entire site, and so on…" and "What kind of screens will the average user of my movie have?"

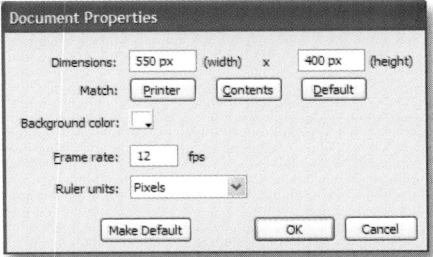

When you know this, you can decide on the best dimensions for your movie. Be sure to always build movies for the least common denominator of your target audience. This ensures that everyone will be included. It also can be tough to resize a document after you'-done the work, so take some time and choose your size carefully.

   CLUNKY MAC PLAYBACK

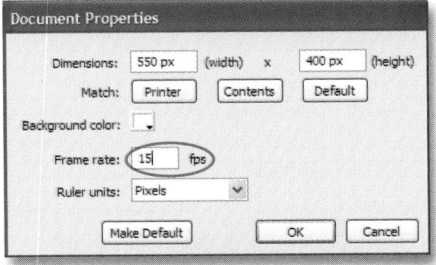

For whatever reason, Flash movies have always played significantly slower on a Mac than Windows. I've heard all types of explanations, but it doesn't really matter why. The fact is that the same SWF will play back slower on a Mac. That being said, the Flash 7 player does a much better job of bringing both platforms to an equal speed than any previous player.

So what can you do about this? Unfortunately, not much. I would recommend setting all your movies to play back at 15fps. This will make sure that on a Mac, you'll at least get 12fps. The results are just too unpredictable, so I would also suggest testing every movie you intend to publish on a Mac before actually launching it. That's the only way to really be sure. At least Macromedia acknowledges the speed difference. Does that make you feel better? Yeah, me neither.

   BRIGHTNESS FADES TOO

Optimizing your final movie is a very important part of the process. After all, you want to make sure everyone can view your content without problems. If you really want to nit-pick and tune perform-ance, try this one on for size.

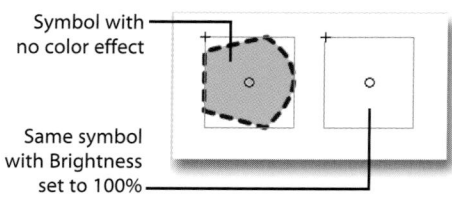

Symbol with no color effect

Same symbol with Brightness set to 100%

Normally, creating a fade effect would require you to set the Alpha effect for one of the instances. However, you can set the Brightness effect (in the Property inspector) to accomplish the same goal. Setting the brightness to 100 will turn the instance com-pletely white, and setting it to –100 will turn it black. If you have a white or black background for your movie, it can appear as though the symbol has disappeared. The advantage is that the brightness effect is much less processor-intensive than Alpha. If you make this change for several fades, you can really speed things up, especially if you have several complex fades. This won't be applicable every time, but try it and see if it works for what you're doing. Talk about your fine-tuning!

   FLASH IS FOR THE WEB, RIGHT?

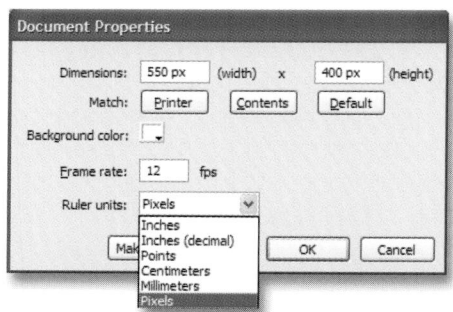

Not anymore. With each release of Flash, Macromedia offers more and more to people who intend to use Flash for presentations, video, and print. Flash 2004 is no different. In fact, some might say this release is the most aggressive yet in catering to those purposes. Open your document properties (CTRL-J), and at the bottom you'll see a new drop-down that lists different ruler units. The default is pixels, but you can easily change to inches, which makes more sense when publishing print materials.

If you've used Illustrator, Photoshop, or Fireworks (to name a few), this will not sound too impressive. However, for Flash, this is a long-awaited and helpful option that lets designers work with other mediums in mind, not just the web.

WHY'S MY FILE SO BIG?

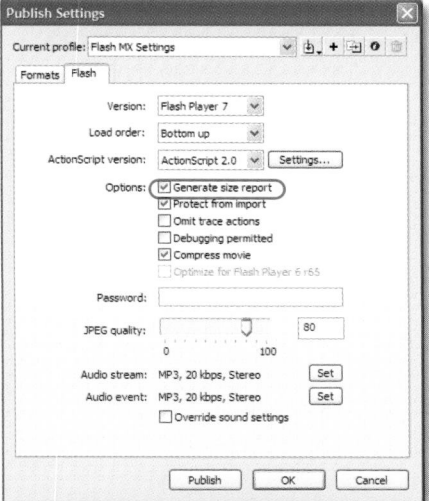

Have you ever published your final movie and almost fainted because of how big your SWF file turned out to be? How did such a simple project turn out to have such a big file? The good news is there's a way to find out just that.

In your document's Publish Settings (CTRL-SHIFT-F12 or OPT-SHIFT-F12 on the Mac), go to the Flash tab. Put a check next to the box that says "Generate Size Report" and Publish your movie. The Output window will open and show you a detailed run-down of how many bytes each asset in your movie contributes to the overall size. You'll also find a new text file in the directory where your SWF is published with the same information stored there.

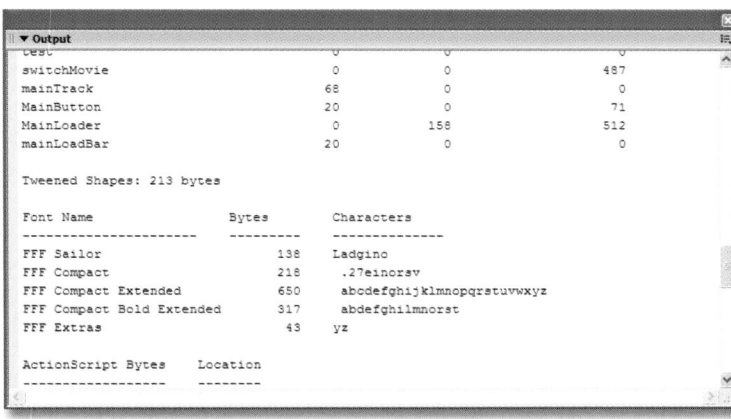

I'll tell you right now that most of the times when I generate these things, I find that a font is the culprit. Whoever the bad guy is, you'll find him here for sure.

  AHHH, FRAME RATES

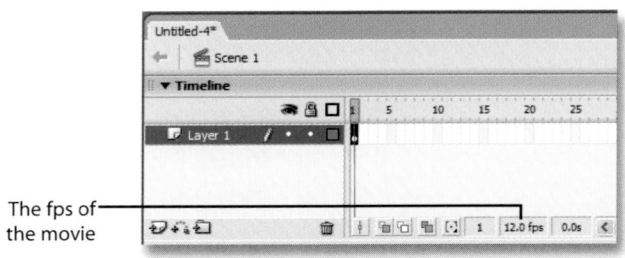

The fps of the movie

Choosing the right frame rate for a Flash movie can be a tricky proposition. There's so much to consider. If you want a universal answer, though, go with 12 (Flash default). It's going to work for just about every situation. If you want a better answer than that, you'll need to choose a rate that is going to be the best for your audience. It also depends on what kind of content you are publishing. For example, if you are publishing to a QuickTime video file for use in video production, you'll want to set your frame rate to 30fps. Here are some of my recommendations:

Content	Audience	FPS
Basic animation	Low-end web user	12
Basic animation/ interactivity	Average web user	15
Timed scripting/ basic animation	High-end web user	20
Broadcast video	Video editor	24/30

Of course, these are just recommendations. You should determine your ideal frame rate by testing your content for your audience. If all else fails, fall back on 12.

   BETTER SAVE THAN SORRY

I know it's a really old cliché, but how do you think clichés get to be clichés? Let me tell you a story that happened to me early in my Flash experiences. I was working on a project (one file) and saved over and over again for hours at a time. It took me weeks to finish the project, and I constantly saved my work to be safe. One morning, I opened my file and got an error: "Unrecognized File Format." I tried again. I tried reinstalling Flash. I rebooted. I tried another computer. Nothing. For some reason, the file had become corrupt. My work was lost forever. Here's what I recommend. As you work, make constant backups by saving as a new file each time you make major changes. Keep them organized by using a number system like this: "MyProject_100.fla," "MyProject_101.fla," and so on. It's like putting a version number at the end of every filename. If something goes wrong, you always have a recent backup to revert to. Trust me on this one.

 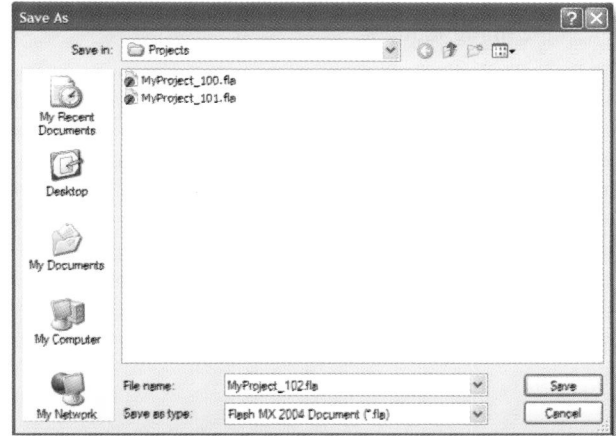

  FLASH FORECASTING

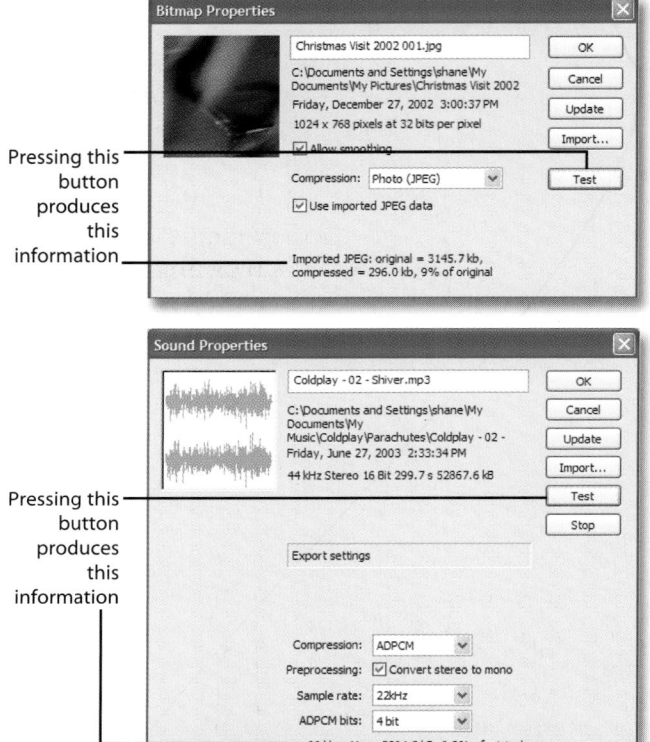

Pressing this button produces this information

Pressing this button produces this information

Often, when we work with sounds and images, we are not quite sure how much they'll add to our final file size. This is especially true if we're recompressing them using Flash settings. Well, this doesn't have to be a mystery.

Double-click any image or sound in your Library and, in the Properties window, you'll see a Test button. If you press it, you'll be given information under the compression settings about the size of the asset in question. You can then change the settings and test again to see the effects. Not only do you get this mini-report on file size, but you also get a preview of the output. If you are testing a sound, the sound will play for you, and if you're testing an image, you'll get a mini-preview in the top-left corner of the window. Use this tip to help you determine the best individual settings to balance quality and file size.

   I HAVE INDIVIDUAL QUALITIES

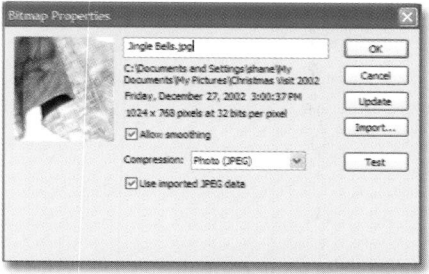

Having multiple images and sounds in your document is not uncommon. Typically, all these imported assets have Flash default compression settings applied to them. That's great if you want everything to look or sound the same. Let's say you have ten short rollover sounds and one track of music in your document. It's much more important that the music play back in good quality than the rollover sounds that are heard only for a brief moment.

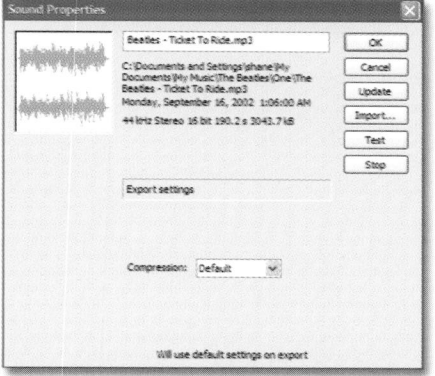

Because every asset can have an individual purpose, it only makes sense that each would get its own settings as well. If you double-click any image or sound in the Library, you'll be given individual compression settings. Depending on the type of file you imported, the default can be different. Regardless, you can change them on an individual basis and give them a sense of individuality. It's too bad certain people I know don't have these settings. Then again, maybe they do. I'll have to check.

   LOW ON RESOURCES

Don't have the latest computer hardware available? Have to run one program at a time so the thing doesn't chug, chug, chug away? Not to worry, you may be able to get Flash running a bit faster if you clear its History every once in a while. This is especially helpful if you have been working for a while on several different files, which results in several histories existing in memory. Clear the history of a document quickly by opening the panel (ALT-F10 or OPT-F10 on Mac) and going to the panel menu (top-right corner) to choose Clear History. It's kind of like clearing your browser cache, except that everything in these histories is in memory instead of on your disk so they can slow you down quite a bit. Hopefully things will speed up a bit after that. If not, you may want to save up for a newer system.

  BROKEN BITMAPS

Have you imported bitmaps, placed them on your Stage, and run into some strange visual problem or defect? There have been times when a bitmap does something unpredictable. This may be due to the way you're placing the bitmap on the Stage. You can place an

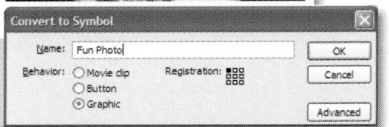

image on the Stage by dragging the bitmap symbol from the Library, but it's better to do it this way….

Convert the bitmap to raw artwork using Modify > Break Apart (CTRL-B). If the bitmap is inside a symbol, edit the symbol and break it apart there. Having the image broken apart ensures that it is displayed clearly and properly. Don't ask me why, because I think either way should work equally well. However, this is the method recommended by Macromedia as well as myself. That means you better listen. Pretty please?

   CUSTOM UNDOS?

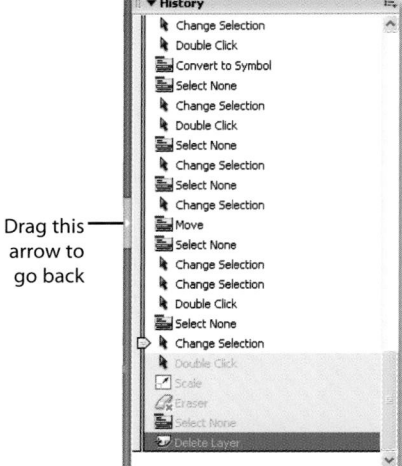

Drag this arrow to go back

The History panel (ALT-F10) has made a big impact in Flash MX 2004. Along with all the other tricks it introduced that we discuss elsewhere, you can also undo several actions at once with a simple drag. With the History panel open, simply slide the little wedge on the left side of the action list up until you get to the last action you would like to leave as performed. You'll see the changes taking place on your Stage or Timeline as you drag the slider. Then you can just begin working again and it will overwrite the actions you undid. Doing things this way keeps you more informed as to what specifically you're undoing instead of just pressing CTRL-Z over and over and watching what changes. That's the way I used to do things, but no more. From now on, it's the History panel all the way.

   BACK AND FORTH, TO AND FRO

Clients of mine would constantly voice this complaint: "Flash is great, but people can't use their browser's back button to navigate through a Flash site or movie." My response was, "You're ugly!" Then Flash MX introduced Named Anchors, enabling me to stop insulting clients.

To see how this works, create a layer called "anchors" and create a keyframe every 10 frames. Select the first keyframe and type "anchor1" in the Frame field of the Property inspector, change the label type to Anchor, and repeat these steps for the other keyframes, changing the name of the anchor to something unique for each one. Create another layer, placing keyframes that match those on the first layer, but instead of anchors, put different

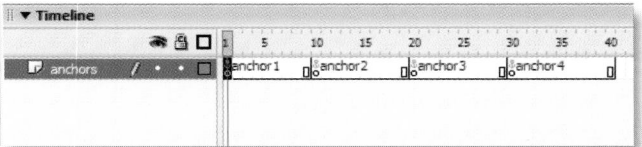

artwork on each keyframe. Finally, put a stop action on the last keyframe so that the movie plays only once.

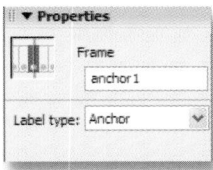

Open the document's Publish Settings (CTRL-SHIFT-F12 or OPT-SHIFT-F12 on the Mac) and, on the HTML tab, change the template to "Flash with Named Anchors." Now publish your movie and open the HTML page that was created in a browser window. As the movie plays, you'll see that the browser's back button becomes active. After it's done, you can press the back button, and it will jump the Flash movie to each named anchor that you defined on the Timeline without unloading the Flash movie itself. Of course, the Forward button will also work once you press back a few times.

Think of it like a bookmarking system for your Flash Timeline. You can save history points and let the user jump through them as they would an HTML site.

  FLASHENATE THE IMAGE

Do you like the word I made up? "Image." Yeah, I have hundreds of them. When you Flashenate an image, you're actually converting it from raster to vector artwork. Many programs do this, but Flash does it so well, there's almost no need to use any of the others.

Select any bitmap image on the Stage and go to Modify > Bitmap > Trace Bitmap. If you set the options here higher, you'll get vector art that is more like the original image, where lower settings create more distortion. The advantage to low settings is that it saves file size and converts quickly. You can leave the settings alone and click OK to see the effect.

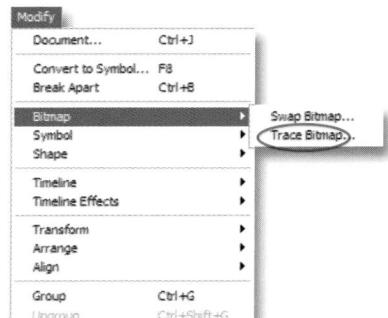

I often Trace Bitmaps to create stylized graphics or to reduce file size when there are a lot of images. The only problem is that tracing a very complex vector image can actually increase the file size, so be careful and test each option to find what's right for you.

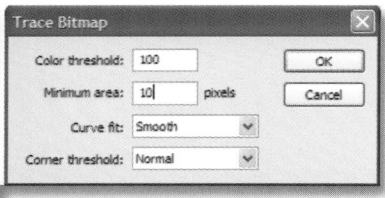

SCALING WOES

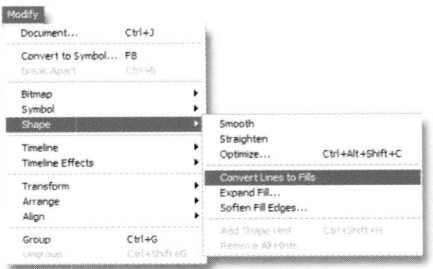

From time to time, you may draw some artwork that is rather complex. On top of that, you may animate these drawings or scale them down to miniature sizes. This can cause some of these drawings to look a little crude or even slow down the animation on slower computers. Select the shape in question (strokes and fills), go to Modify, then Shape, and then choose Convert Lines to Fills. Doing so will convert selected lines to filled shapes, which can speed up drawing for some animations and make very small, complex drawings easier to see. This might not always be the best thing though, because it can increase your file size. I'll leave it up to you to find the best balance. I know what you're thinking: "There's always a tradeoff!" Ain't it the truth?

Converted to fills

   ## PIXEL CLEAR

A growing number of designers are starting to use pixel fonts. You know these fonts, right? Like when you go to a site and the text is small and crystal clear? These are pixel fonts, and they can be found at sites such as `www.orgdot.com`, `www.atomicmedia.net`, and `www.fontsforflash.com`. I'll admit, I like these things too, and you'll see them in a lot of my designs (if you care to look). You may have used these fonts and found that they turn out blurry for you. Well, that's because these little guys have to be used a certain way.

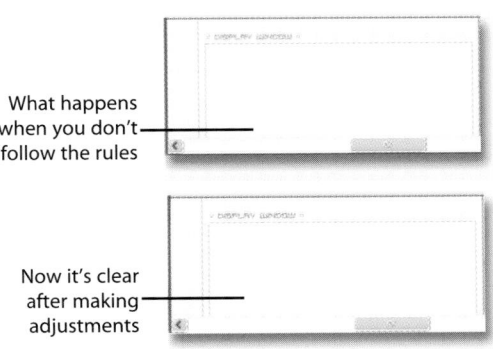

What happens when you don't follow the rules

Now it's clear after making adjustments

When using a pixel font, look at the Property inspector to make sure you have positioned the text field on a whole pixel. This means that instead of putting something at X: 1.4, Y: 5.8, you'd put it at X: 1.0, Y: 6.0. You must also make sure that if you put text in a symbol, the symbol also lands on a whole pixel. There are a few rules to follow as well. For a complete list of the rules, look on the web site where you got the font from. Hey, rules are rules.

   10,000 LEAGUES OF UNDO

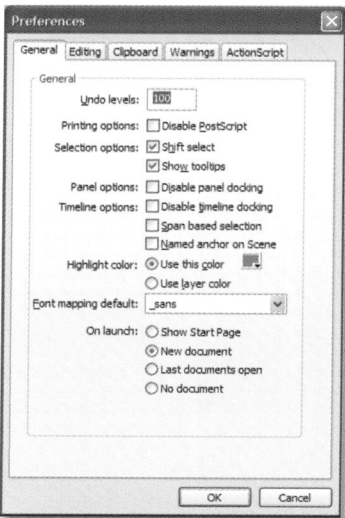

We're human beings, and as such, we make mistakes. Some of us make more than others, although I don't makE any… oops! Of course, Flash takes this into account and gives you the ability to undo the things you do in a document. However, by default you're only allowed 100 actions before Flash begins to forget what you did. Okay, 100 is a lot, but that may be the point. Every undo allowed takes up memory, so if you have a computer with limited resources, or if you just want to be able to make more mistakes, Flash can accommodate you. In your Flash preferences (CTRL-U or Flash Preferences) under the General tab there is a box for you to specify the number of Undo levels you'd like to allow for. Enter any number from 2 to 9999 that you feel best suits your needs. I use 2, wink, wink.

   CLEANING HOUSE, OR THE LIBRARY

Okay, so you've been importing graphics, creating buttons, and converting things to movie clips for hours. You've changed your animations so much that you can't remember what they were supposed to be when you started. Now when you look at your Library, it's filled with tons of stuff, and you're not sure if you're using even half of it. If you're like me, you like to run a tight ship and want all unused materials destroyed. Luckily, the Library has a nifty feature that tells you if an asset is being used anywhere in the movie.

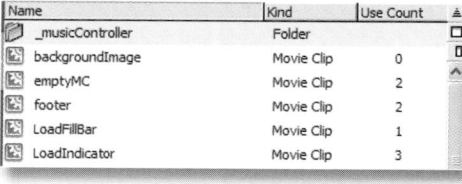

Click the panel menu at the top right of the Library and put a check by Keep Use Counts Updated. Next, expand the Library by clicking the middle of the three buttons above the Library's vertical scrollbar. You can now see the number of times each asset is being used and delete any unused item. Be sure to turn off this feature when you're done because it does use processing power. Be warned that if you are attaching movies using linkage settings and ActionScript, this feature will not identify them as being used. It only recognizes them when they are physically placed on the Stage.

   TRIM THE FAT

I'm not talking about a visit to the plastic surgeon here (although often our projects could use a little liposuction). If your files are getting out of hand, go to your Library, open the Panel menu, and choose "Select Unused Items." This will automatically select every asset in your Library that does not have an instance placed on a Timeline somewhere.

You may need to do this a few times to get all of them because removing one item that has another unused item will make all those items that are on its Timeline unused.

Be careful, though. If you are attaching any movies using ActionScript, this method will count them as unused because they aren't physically placed anywhere. I'd recommend keeping these assets in special folders so that you don't grab the wrong ones.

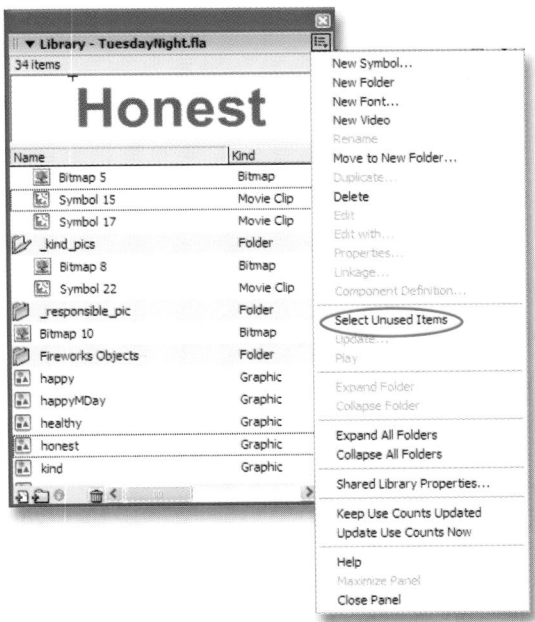

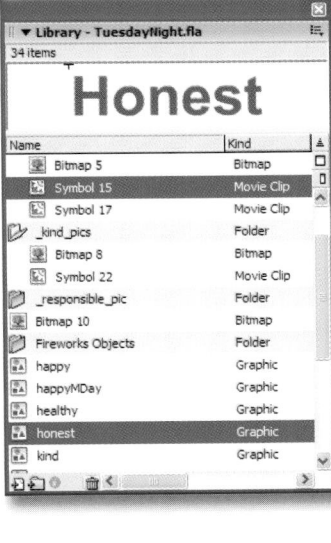

   TOO SMOOTH FOR ME

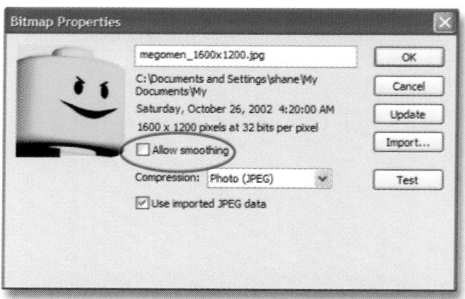

Any time you import a bitmap into a document, a secret option is set that you may not even be aware of. It's called smoothing, and it can actually make your images a little blurry and unclear. Here's how to take things into your own hands.

Locate a bitmap in the Library and double-click it. Here you'll see the check box for smoothing. For whatever reason, it's always enabled by default, but disabling it will retain definition and clarity of the imported image. Smoothing is really only useful for certain GIF images that can import with jagged edges, so you may want to disable this for every image you use.

There are many cases where having smoothing on or off makes such a small difference that you can't even tell, so figure out what's best for you and stick with it. For me, I like turning it off whenever I can.

   NULL SOUND

You may have many sounds and music tracks in your Timeline that you want to sync up with your animations. Although we've already discussed how to do this using the Stream sound method for an individual sound, the drawback to that method can be an increased file size. To force all your sounds (even Event sounds) into Streaming mode while reducing file size by about 90%, you can use the Null sound method.

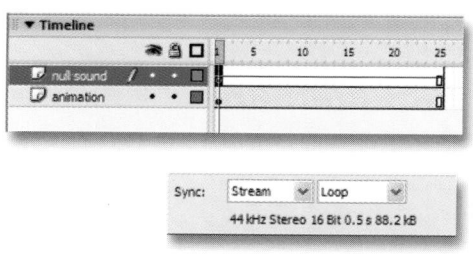

Create a .wav or .aif sound file called null.wav or null.aif that is 0.1 seconds long and import it into Flash. This can be done with any sound editor. Place this null sound on its own layer in the Timeline you want to keep in sync and set the sound to Stream instead of Event. Now set it to Loop. Doing this keeps all the animation in sync with the sounds, and even Event sounds on the same Timeline will be thrown into Streaming mode. Check out a full tutorial at www.vrprofessionals.com/html/whitepaper/nullsound.htm.

REDUCE YOUR CURVES

A lot of times, the things we draw are not so smooth and end up being fairly complex if we're not careful. Here's a way to minimize these problems.

Select any shape with a number of curves in it and go to Modify > Shape > Optimize (CTRL-ALT-SHIFT-C or CMD-SHIFT-OPT-C on Mac). This reduces the number of curves used, which results in smoother and less complex shapes. The major benefit here is a reduction in file size. Obviously you'd have to optimize many complex shapes to see huge savings, but if you're counting every byte, then add this to your list of optimizing techniques.

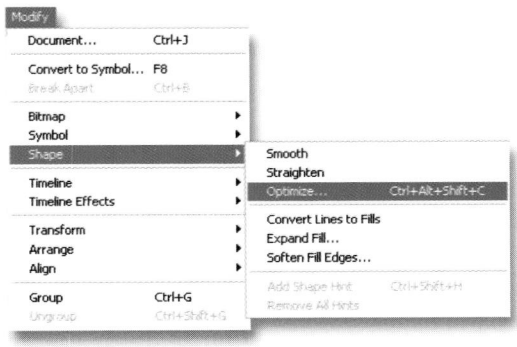

Checking "Use Multiple Passes" will repeat the process until no more optimization is possible. It's the same as doing it manually over and over.

As a warning, the higher you set the smoothing setting when optimizing, the less like the original outline your shape will look. Also, your results depend on the outline selected, but play with this one and see if it helps you create smoother and smaller movies.

DON'T ALWAYS BE SO CINEMATIC

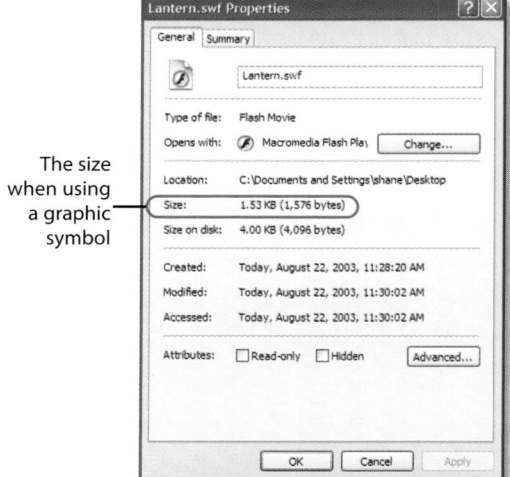

The size when using a graphic symbol

The size when using a movie clip

The number-one way to reduce file size in Flash is to create symbols out of objects that you use repeatedly. The only thing they leave out when mentioning this rule is that all symbol types are not created equal. When I first started, I would just convert everything to movie clip symbols. The problem is movie clips have many more properties and capabilities than graphic symbols. The extra information stored for each movie clip is very small, but can add up to significantly larger files. This is especially true if you have hundreds of symbols and they're all movie clips.

The solution is to create graphic symbols when you can. If you don't need specific properties that movie clips offer, then don't use them. To determine which to use, I ask myself, "Will there be an animation in the symbol?" If the answer's no, then I create a graphic symbol. The great thing is that you can always convert your symbols from one to the other, so you're not stuck with any decision.

SOUND THAT SYNCS

If you have an animation that needs to be synchronized to music or a voice file, you may get frustrated. On your computer, it's in total sync, but on someone else's, things are a bit off. Try putting the entire animation on one Timeline and then putting your sound on a

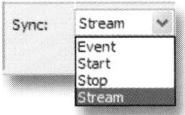

separate layer on the same Timeline. Now select the keyframe that the sound is on, look to the Property inspector, and where it says Sync, change it from Event to Stream. Doing this will force the animation to play in sync with the audio on the same Timeline. Frames in the animation will be dropped if necessary so that the sound and animation frames will always play in tandem.

The only thing you have to worry about is that the sound layer must now have enough frames to play completely. Keep extending the frames of the sound layer if you need to until the entire sound plays back.

EXECUTE FLASH

If you work with Flash long enough, you're bound to run into some problems with the plug-in. In general, plug-ins are not perfect, and Flash is no different. The frustrating thing is that sometimes it seems as though these problems won't go away. If you're like me where friends and family constantly call you (because your middle name is "tech-support"), then you've likely run into this one… "Suddenly, when I go to a Flash web site, the plug-in is not detected or the content doesn't play at all. I have the latest version. What do I do?" Well, here's a quick fix for the problems you just can't figure out (with the plug-in, that is).

Have the person go to the following:

`www.macromedia.com/support/flash/ts/documents/remove_player.htm`

Macromedia has provided an uninstaller to safely remove the Flash plug-in. They even provide instructions on how to do it manually if the uninstaller doesn't work. Usually after removing the player and then re-installing it from scratch, everything returns to normal. Not many people know about this one, so keep it on the down low!

INDEX

inform**IT**

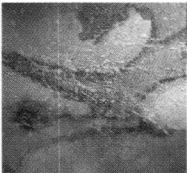

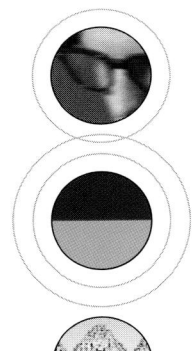
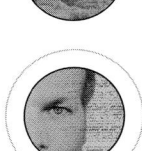

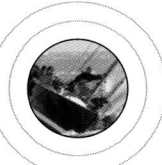

VOICES THAT MATTER

VISIT OUR WEB SITE

WWW.NEWRIDERS.COM

On our Web site you'll find information about our other books, authors, tables of contents, indexes, and book errata. You will also find information about book registration and how to purchase our books.

EMAIL US

Contact us at this address: **nrfeedback@newriders.com**

- If you have comments or questions about this book
- To report errors that you have found in this book
- If you have a book proposal to submit or are interested in writing for New Riders
- If you would like to have an author kit sent to you
- If you are an expert in a computer topic or technology and are interested in being a technical editor who reviews manuscripts for technical accuracy

- To find a distributor in your area, please contact our international department at this address. **nrmedia@newriders.com**

- For instructors from educational institutions who want to preview New Riders books for classroom use. Email should include your name, title, school, department, address, phone number, office days/hours, text in use, and enrollment, along with your request for desk/examination copies and/or additional information.
- For members of the media who are interested in reviewing copies of New Riders books. Send your name, mailing address, and email address, along with the name of the publication or Web site you work for.

BULK PURCHASES/CORPORATE SALES

The publisher offers discounts on this book when ordered in quantity for bulk purchases and special sales. For sales within the U.S., please contact: Corporate and Government Sales (800) 382-3419 or **corpsales@pearsontechgroup.com**. Outside of the U.S., please contact: International Sales (317) 428-3341 or **international@pearsontechgroup.com**.

WRITE TO US

New Riders Publishing
800 East 96th Street, 3rd Floor
Indianapolis, IN 46240

CALL US

Toll-free (800) 571-5840. Ask for New Riders.
If outside U.S. (317) 428-3000. Ask for New Riders.

FAX US

(317) 428-3280

New Riders

VIEW CART ⛟   [   ] search ⊙

▸ Registration already a member? Log in. ▸ Book Registration

OUR AUTHORS

PRESS ROOM

EDUCATORS

ABOUT US

CONTACT US

| ∷ web development | ∷ design | ∷ photoshop | ∷ new media | ∷ 3-D | ∷ server technologies |

You already know that New Riders brings you the **Voices that Matter**. But what does that mean? It means that New Riders brings you the Voices that challenge your assumptions, take your talents to the next level, or simply help you better understand the complex technical world we're all navigating.

Visit **www.newriders.com** to find:

▸ *Discounts* on specific book purchases

▸ Never before published chapters

▸ Sample chapters and excerpts

▸ Author bios and interviews

▸ Contests and enter-to-wins

▸ Up-to-date industry event information

▸ Book reviews

▸ Special offers from our friends and partners

▸ Info on how to join our User Group program

▸ Ways to have your Voice heard

New
Riders

W W W . N E W R I D E R S . C O M

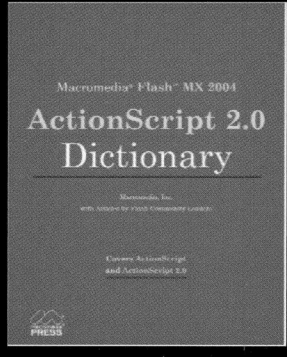